Praise for *The End of the* P9-ELO-923

"Searing. . . . It stays with you. . . . [Goolrick is] a gifted writer with a memorable account of his terribly flawed family."
—*USA Today*

"Reads like a novel. . . . [Goolrick] tells a story which is fascinating, if terribly sad, but which is lightened by unexpected moments of humor. . . . And be forewarned, no one I know has finished this book with dry eyes."
—Nancy Pearl, commentator for NPR's *Morning Edition*

"Unnerving, elegantly crafted. . . . Morbidly funny."
—*Entertainment Weekly*

"Clear, forceful. . . . An exquisite memoir that everyone should read." —*Minneapolis Star Tribune*

"A courageous and successful work." —*People*

"Anecdotes of captivating vitality. . . . *The End of the World as We Know It* is barbed and canny, with a sharp eye for the infliction of pain." —*The New York Times*

"Indelible. . . . A devastatingly shrewd no-nonsense description of mid-20th century Southern mores and manners that can rank with the work of Walker Percy or Peter Taylor."
—Newsweek.com

"Magnificent. Hypnotically candid and beautifully written. . . .
Singular."   —Haven Kimmel, author of *A Girl Named Zippy*

"A devastating debut. . . . Worthy of William Styron and Flannery O'Connor. . . . Goolrick is clearly a victim of his parents' brutal abuse, but he has broken out of the categories of 'victim' and 'survivor' to become a powerful truth-teller."

—*Kirkus Reviews*, starred

"Searing. . . . Heartbreakingly intimate. . . . Breathtaking honesty."   —*Richmond Times-Dispatch*

"[A] blistering family memoir."   —*Seattle Post-Intelligencer*

"Robert Goolrick is a huge, shining talent."
—Martin Clark, author of *Plain Heathen Mischief*

"Brilliant. . . . A brief yet powerful record of long familial dysfunction."   —*The Raleigh News & Observer*

"Sharp, searing. . . . The events of *The End of the World as We Know It* jump off the page with unforgettable vitality. . . . It reminds readers why one man's unflinching truth still matters, still demands the printed page."   —Bookslut.com

"Raw, impassioned, terrifying. . . . To say that it's the story of life in an alcoholic household in Virginia would be like calling *A Streetcar Named Desire* a play about a lonely woman. It catches the premise but not the development or the dramatic power."

—*Palm Beach Post*

THE
END OF
THE WORLD
AS WE
KNOW IT

SCENES FROM A LIFE

Robert Goolrick

Algonquin Books of Chapel Hill 2008

Published by

ALGONQUIN BOOKS OF CHAPEL HILL

Post Office Box 2225

Chapel Hill, North Carolina 27515-2225

a division of

WORKMAN PUBLISHING

225 Varick Street

New York, New York 10014

First paperback edition, Algonquin Books of Chapel Hill, April 2008.
Originally published by Algonquin Books of Chapel Hill in 2007.
Printed in the United States of America.
Published simultaneously in Canada by Thomas Allen & Son Limited.
Design by Anne Winslow.

Library of Congress Cataloging-in-Publication Data
Goolrick, Robert, 1948–
    The end of the world as we know it : scenes from a life /
Robert Goolrick.—1st ed.
        p. cm.
    ISBN-13: 978-1-56512-481-3 (HC)
    1. Goolrick, Robert, 1948–   2. Problem families—United States—
Biography.   3. Interpersonal relations—United States.   I. Title.
CT275.G587A3 2007
973.92092—dc22
[B]   2006047632
ISBN-13: 978-1-56512-602-2 (PB)

10 9 8 7 6 5 4 3 2 1
First Paperback Edition

FOR LYNN GROSSMAN AND BOB BALABAN,

who said there would be a book,

and

THOMAS KALMAN,

who said there would be time

Come death, and with thy fingers close my eyes,
Or if I live, let me forget myself.

CHRISTOPHER MARLOWE, *Edward II*

THE
END OF
THE WORLD
AS WE
KNOW IT

Both Now and Forever

I

My father died because he drank too much. Six years before, my mother had died because she drank too much. I drank too much. The apple doesn't fall very far from the tree.

My father was cremated. My mother was cremated, too. When she died on Labor Day, six years before, my father was too weak with grief to go through with a burial service, so my mother's ashes sat on a shelf in the funeral home for months, until the next spring, when suddenly one day my father got her ashes and had the yard man bury her in the back yard, in a little garden just off the back terrace where we sit sometimes in the evenings watching the creek and feeling the cool breeze off the water.

My mother's grave went unmarked, and nobody knew quite where she was, and my aunt was frantic with worry that there had been no burial service, no proper Episcopal blessing. The following Christmas, we gave my father a cast-iron statue of a unicorn—my mother had always loved them—and we put the statue approximately on the spot where she was buried. We put the statue on top of a marble pastry board from the kitchen.

My father was probably the only man in history to receive a funerary statue as a Christmas present. It came in a crate as big as a washing machine, and he opened it on Christmas morning, just like it was a new set of golf clubs or something.

It wasn't a funeral, not a real one, but at least her ashes weren't sitting with a bunch of strangers in the funeral home anymore. My mother never allowed us to use the word *home,* or *drapes* or *shrubs,* or *Mom* or *gift* or *kids,* she thought it was tacky, but I don't know what else to call a place where they keep people's ashes after they've been cremated.

My sister and I decided to bury my father next to my mother, or where we thought my mother was, underneath the unicorn, and to have a burial service for both of them, so my mother's soul would finally be free to go to heaven, to cease her endless wandering limbo in the ecclesiastical ether, and this pleased my aunt a lot. It was almost legal, to bury your parents in the back yard.

The house my father lived in, which I owned, was a wreck. Six months before, I had been home for a visit with him, and I woke up in the night and heard something moving in the room. When I turned on the light, there were three enormous rats on the crappy rug, sniffing at my garden clothes that I had tossed in a corner to be washed. I threw a book at them, and they scurried into wherever they lived, but it kind of freaked me out, so I went downstairs to sleep on the sofa. At dawn, I woke up again, to find two rats fucking on the Persian rug—we never said carpet, not even when it was wall-to-wall—so I sat up and threw an ashtray at them, and then stayed awake, rigid with fury, until my father came down to breakfast.

"This can't go on," I said. "There are rats fucking on my mother's Persian rug and it can't go on another day."

He didn't even answer, just went on cooking his eggs and bacon as though I weren't even in the room. That was his reaction to anything unpleasant, to pretend it wasn't happening, so I called an exterminator, who came out that day. He took one sniff in the sitting room and said, "You have a serious infestation problem." That was exactly what he said. He was so serious, like a doctor telling you that you had a fatal disease. "This could take a year."

By the time my father died, on August 15, the rats were practically gone, at least they didn't run around in the daytime, although the house smelled a lot like dead rats, if you kept the doors closed.

When I got into the house, I called my sister, whom I love very much. "We're orphans now," I said. "Who's going to adopt a forty-three-year-old orphan?" Then I started to get ready for the funeral.

My father had a carport. Just saying carport gives me a vague feeling of nausea. He had bought it from Sears, and it was just big enough to get his Chevy Nova under cover. His Chevy Nova stank to high heaven because the previous summer, my father had put the garbage in the trunk to take to the Dumpster, and then he forgot and left it there for six weeks, until I came home and got into the car and gagged and looked in the trunk and took the six-week-old summer garbage to the Dumpster. I sold the car eight years later, and it never stopped stinking. But the carport really bugged me.

There it sat, corrugated tin on flimsy poles, in front of the two-hundred-year-old house that my grandmother had bought seventy years before. So the first thing I did was call the yard man, who was named Claudie, and ask him to come out and cut the grass, because I knew there would be a lot of people coming to the house in the following days and at least the yard would look decent. While he was there I asked him to take down the carport and throw it away. This was the day after my father's death and already the carport was going, and Claudie asked if he could have it and I said sure, so he carefully took it apart and loaded it into his truck, which anybody could see would never fit into the carport anyway, so I was puzzled, but I was just glad to have the thing gone.

He probably had other cars. Some people in Virginia like to leave used cars in their yards as though they were extra pieces of real estate.

We cleaned the house, my sister, my aunt, and I, until late in the night. We cleaned at least the parts where people might go. There were plates of food still left on the kitchen counter and the kitchen floor for the dog to eat, mostly Styrofoam containers from places like Long John Silver's. My aunt kept singing this sort of little song over and over—"Greasy cobwebs," she would sing cheerily, as she attacked the ceiling with a broom, "Greasy cobwebs."

Much later, I learned that both she and my uncle despised my father, whom I had supposed to be universally liked, he had been so charming, at least until he became a total recluse who only went to town at eight-thirty in the morning to get the mail and go to the library for stacks of mystery novels and to buy his dinner at some fast-food place, some greasy something which would sit out all day until he heated it up at night and took three bites.

He must have been so lonely.

When we were done cleaning, the house didn't look great, but at least the sitting room and the dining room looked OK. The dining room had once been in another room, but my father had all the furniture removed and moved his bed in there so he didn't have to walk up the stairs drunk every night.

That was the other thing I did the day after my father died. I took apart the bed he slept in and gave it to my sister. It had been the bed she slept in as a child, a little twin bed, and my father had passed most of his hours on it, reading an endless number of mystery stories and watching TV and talking to his dog, Sam Weller, and drinking bourbon. My sister would go out and cut his toenails in that room. He bathed and went to the bathroom in the old pantry, where he had had a sink and toilet and tin shower installed, the only bathroom in the world that had been put together without any heating at all, so the pipes froze every winter and I suppose he had to go upstairs then, at least once in a while.

The day after my father died, my godfather's wife appeared with a ham. There was one slice taken out of the middle of it. "We just had this ham left over, and thought maybe you could use it," she said, as though it were an ordinary thing to go to all the trouble to cook a ham for eight hours in the middle of the summer, and as though one missing slice relegated it to the land of leftovers. It was an act of enormous kindness, done in perfect taste, and I appreciated it. People followed her, and they brought all kinds of food, with instructions pinned to the wax paper telling us how long to heat it up at 350. Grief, I suppose, makes you hungry, and since it was way too hot to cook anything, we ate whatever came to the door. A lot of it was really good.

Also, the day after my father died, this eighteen-year-old kid appeared out of nowhere and stood in the yard. He was from one of the houses up the hill, and he said that my father's dog, a black Labrador who was dumber than dirt, but sweet, had taken to wandering into his yard and he had started feeding him. Sam Weller wasn't thin, living, as he did, on a steady diet of Long John Silver's and Arby's and so on. The kid told me he was going off to Vanderbilt in the fall. "That's a good school," I said.

"Can I have your father's dog?" he asked. I thought about it a long time, wondering at the gall that had made him walk into a grief-stricken yard and start asking for dogs—I mean this was a sweet, good-natured dog he was asking for—but I knew that after I went back to New York I would visit the house only occasionally, and my sister already had two dogs and two children, and so I said yes. The kid didn't even know the dog's name, so I told him, and he stared at me blankly, and I figured there would be a lot for him to learn at Vanderbilt. I told him he could have the dog and he whistled and Sam came trotting over and the boy led him away, up through the woods, and that was the last time I ever saw that dog.

People came. My brother and his wife came from Atlanta, but they stayed in a motel, as they always did. Unexpected people came. Even two friends of mine from New York came, flying down in bad weather to stand up in a church and pay respects to a man they didn't know, just to be a comfort to me. It touched my heart.

Old friends of my father's came, and they would sit in the rat-free sitting room and have cocktails or iced tea and talk about my father. They told a lot of funny stories. There are more tears at the average Southern wedding than the average Southern funeral, and this was pretty much the case with my father. A lot of the stories had to do with times my father had gotten drunk and done funny things or said funny things, or when other people had gotten drunk and been hilarious, the life of the party. And there were the usual outpourings of melancholy. My father had been much loved.

The sitting room was very pretty, but there wasn't a single comfortable chair in the whole room, all the furniture was so cheap, bought on the quick without any care or thought, mismatched, everything, so they didn't stay long. Besides which, it was very hot, and we didn't have any air-conditioning.

My brother isn't very good at grief, he avoids scenes that trouble him, but he was very useful because he could sit for hours trading anecdotes with the people who came to visit. He's sort of the king of anecdotes, and he's very witty. Actually, he's kind of like my father, although he's never drunk.

The richest woman in the state of Virginia came, driving all the way up from the Eastern shore, bringing a bucket of tomatoes from the farm, as she called it, an immense Georgian mansion and something like three thousand acres on the Rappahannock.

After a Southern funeral, you always have people out to the

house for drinks and lunch, if it's in the morning, and my father's was going to be at eleven, so we called a caterer, the only one in town, and she said she'd put together some chicken salad on rolls and sliced ham, which we had plenty of, and things like that, so people would have something to eat. It was hot as blazes.

People kept asking me if there was anything they could do, if there was some way they could help, and I kept saying no, partially because I was such a control freak and partially because I really couldn't think of anything. We had cleaned up the house and cleared out my father's room. We had put his few junky clothes in boxes to be thrown away, and we'd put the dining room table back in there, and the chairs, so it looked pretty much the way it always had before my father had retired from the world. My sister and I worked like dogs, which is what you do after somebody dies. Everything was done, so we just sat around, listening to anecdotes and eating ham and going over in the hot afternoons to swim in my sister's pool. The hours seemed languid and long. In times of grief, you're waiting for something to happen, but the thing you're waiting for has already taken place.

The morning of my father's funeral, I woke up at six o'clock and realized that there was one thing that hadn't been done. If my father was going to be buried next to my mother, there wasn't any hole to put him in. Nobody had thought to dig a hole.

Claudie would have done it. Claudie would do anything. But I had forgotten.

So I got out of bed and put on some ripped jeans and an old T-shirt and some Top-Siders and went down and got a shovel and jumped over the wall through the box bushes into the little plot where my mother was buried. (We never said *boxwood bushes*. It was tacky.) I picked up the unicorn statue—it was very heavy and already warm from the heat—and I started to dig in a spot I thought might be next to my mother. I hit the box my mother was buried in, so I shoveled the dirt back over and moved a foot to the right and started digging again. There had been a huge thunderstorm the day before, with torrential rains, and the dirt was wet and caked. It seemed to take a long time, the digging, and I was crying and sweating like a pig because I had drunk so much gin the night before. I was drinking straight out of the bottle by then, and I was pretty much bagged all the time.

I kept measuring the hole with the shovel handle to see if it was deep enough and, when I thought it was, I put the shovel away and went into the kitchen and ate some ham on a roll and had a shot of gin out of the bottle, just to take the edge off, and then I went upstairs and took a bath and shaved and put on my suit and my immaculately polished shoes and wandered around the house, smoking and taking the occasional shot, waiting for my sister and brother-in-law, who were going to take me to the funeral service in the church. My sister pretty much didn't trust me to drive anywhere at any time of the day, and she was right.

When they showed up, I told my brother-in-law I had a question and led him out to the grave I had dug. I asked him if he thought it was deep enough and he said no, so I got the shovel and jumped though the box bushes and started digging again. I dug down about another foot, and when my brother-in-law said that was enough, I put the shovel away and we went to the funeral. The air-conditioning in the car dried the sweat that soaked my shirt.

They always leave spaces for the family to park at funerals, so we parked right in front and went in and sat in the front row, along with my aunt and uncle and my other aunt and uncle, my father's sister and her husband. The funeral was a standard issue funeral service out of the 1928 prayer book, and then it was over and we got up and filed out, surprised at how many people there were, people from all over the state we hadn't seen since we were children. It seemed odd, filing out before everybody else, like a wedding without the bride, but people looked at us sympathetically, and we smiled back at most of them as though nothing were wrong. That's what you do.

Lunch is kind of a blur, but it happened, and people ate chicken salad and sliced tomatoes and ham, and cold melon, and the children grabbed a sandwich and then swam and waded in the creek to cool off. People laughed a lot. People told us what a wonderful man my father was and how much they would miss him. I can't tell you how much I hated my father, but I agreed with all of them anyway, because that's what you do, as well. Anyway, what good would it have done to say it now?

I had thought I would jump for joy when my father died. I had thought the weight of the world would be lifted from my shoulders. Instead, I was overwhelmed with grief, as was my sister, who had genuinely loved him and taken care of him in every way, no matter how creepy he was.

By one o'clock, most of the people, the people who weren't as close to my father as some of the other people, had left, and the minister came, carrying with him the box with my father's ashes in it. He changed into his vestments in the room off the sitting room and then we were ready for the burial part. The ashes to ashes part.

Somehow the family squeezed into the little space inside the box bushes, and the other people stood on the terrace and looked down at us, the children standing on the wall in their bathing suits, rapt with curiosity— the family group, the minister in his cassock and cotta and his stole, holding the gray box that looked basically like a piece of Tupperware.

The minister read the service, which is very short, and he named both my father and my mother, and I could feel my aunt's exhalation of relief and regret for her sister, and then he turned and handed the box to me.

It was surprisingly heavy. I had expected it to be light as the ashes you clean out of the fireplace, light like artificial whipped cream, but it wasn't. I could see bits of bone through the milky plastic. This was my father in my hands. This was the final sum of my history with my father, and I felt the weight, not just of the box, but of the past, the weight of the anger, the weight of the disaster of our relationship. I had thought I had forgiven him.

I didn't know what I was supposed to do with the box, and then I realized I was supposed to put it into the hole I had dug that morning. I knelt down and put the box in the hole. I looked up and saw the stares on the faces of my father's friends, the children craning to get a better view, and I realized it wasn't over.

I began to shove the dirt in the hole with my hands. I felt like crying, but I knew that would just be a mess, and anyway, it was like planting something, and I had planted things a million times. My sister, bless her heart, knelt down beside me, and with her beautiful slender hands, she shoved dirt as well, watching it fall and cover this man she had loved. This man whose toenails she had clipped, whose hair she had cut.

When it was finished and the last of the dirt was mounded over the box in which my father's ashes would lie forever, I took my sister's hand and we stood up. The people on the porch were still staring, and the minister waited patiently to say his blessing. So I turned and stamped down the dirt with my feet, and then I picked up the marble slab and the heavy statue and placed them over the freshly dug hole. Then the minister said the final blessing, the Lord bless us and keep us, the Lord make his face to shine upon us and be gracious unto us, the Lord lift up the light of his countenance and give us peace, both now and forever.

I always tell men who grieve for their fathers that it never turns out to be what you expected. I tell them that, no matter how much you think about it, no matter how deeply you've decided in advance that you know how you will feel when your father dies, the reality is far deeper and stranger than you can imagine.

I always tell people that if you want closure, as people say now, if you want some finality, you should get up at six o'clock in the morning and dig your father's grave. You should shove the dirt over him with your own hands and stamp it down with your English shoes.

But it's not true. It's not true, the thing I tell people about digging the grave and stamping down the dirt.

I had thought the demons would be laid to rest. I had thought the rage and the hatred that Southern men can feel for their fathers, a rage and hatred so old and terrible they can't be described, I had thought it would all be lifted from me and I would feel free.

It wasn't. Not for a day. Not for a goddamned hour.

II

My mother had varices, which is what happens to you when you drink so much your liver can't process the liquor anymore. The blood backs up and begins to seep through the tiny capillaries in your throat, and then down into your stomach, where it causes pernicious anemia. If you have it once, they can cure it, or stop it or whatever, but it means if you ever drink again, you're pretty much going to die.

I carried her in my arms, against her will, out of the hospital, and laid her in the back of my father's car, and took her to a drying out place, but they wouldn't take her because she was too ill. When we sat in the office, she couldn't even sign her own name. They sent her to the hospital at the University of Virginia, and she was there for six weeks before she was even well enough to go to rehab. She stayed for months in rehab, longer than anybody I've ever known, and when she got out she said to me one day, "My life will never be wonderful again."

I understand what she meant. I still think of drinking with a light and a sweetness that in no way resemble the actual circumstances of those days. Except for a few occasions, it was just being rode hard and put away wet, and I wept at my own behavior almost every night. I lost a decade of my life, just lost it, the way you might lose an umbrella on the bus.

My mother tried to stay sober, I guess. I mean she knew her medical condition, even if she didn't understand it, and she'd been in rehab three months and she had heard the lesson over and over and over, but she thought nice people didn't go to AA meetings and my father kept drinking and it was a hopeless cause. She was an elegant and intelligent woman and she hated her life. I don't know why. She was always unhappy, and nothing would mollify her. No amount of love or tenderness or extravagant gifts. Even getting things she'd always wanted, like the house she lived in, didn't change anything. I'm the same way.

One night I was putting dishes away in a china cupboard, low to the floor, and she leaned over me and whispered, "I can smell liquor on your breath." It was venomous.

Hopeless. She began drinking iced tea or Sprite with vodka in it. She began hiding liquor bottles in her sewing basket. She began hiding liquor bottles in her clothes drawers. She set fire to her mattress. I guess her life was wonderful again.

I took her out for a drive in the car. It was a summer evening, early summer, when it's soft and not too hot and the mountains are still crisp and blue in the distance. I stopped the car on the side of a country road and I turned to her and spoke. "I know what you're doing," I said. "We all know what you're doing. And I want you to know it's going to be long and excruciating and I want you to know that none of us has done anything to deserve what you're about to do."

"I'll stop drinking," she said. "I'll stop drinking for you."

"Don't stop for me," I said. "Don't make me responsible. Don't make me the bad guy." I started the car and we drove home.

One time that summer I was down there for a visit, and I was going out for drinks with some friends. I set the table in the kitchen, three mats and napkins and my grandmother's silver. I told my parents I'd be home at seven, we'd always had dinner at seven-thirty, and we'd have dinner at seven-thirty, like always. I got home at five after seven and they'd already finished their supper.

It was the only time I ever exploded with rage at my parents. "I bought you a fucking house," I yelled. "I come home to see you as often as I can. I never take a vacation, never go anywhere else but here. I bring you presents. And you can't wait five fucking minutes to have supper?"

My mother got up and walked out of the room. My father sat there and said nothing, as though he'd been hit by a baseball bat. I served myself some food and ate in silence. Later, when the twilight was coming on and the light was turning blue, I found my mother in the house and asked her to go for a walk in the garden. To look at my aunt's roses. My mother had long since given up on her own roses.

She said she didn't want to go anywhere with me. I said, "Look. This is what happens in real families. They have fights. They make up. They go for a walk in the garden." I lived in New York. That was what New York families did. My mother, who supposedly was not drinking, rose unsteadily to her feet and we headed for the door.

To get to the roses, you had to cross the gravel driveway and, in the middle, my mother fell down and scraped her elbow very badly on the rocks. She tried to get up, but she couldn't, so I picked her up in my arms, she was light as a leaf, and carried her back into the house, up the stairs, and laid her on her bed. She and my father didn't sleep in the same bedroom anymore. My father snored. Maybe that was the reason.

No, the real reason was that my mother would go to sleep around nine and then she'd wake up at midnight and the liquor would be too far away and she couldn't get back to sleep so she'd lie in bed and play solitaire for hours, sometimes all night. Many, many nights, both drunk and sober, I'd lie in bed and listen to the slap of the cards as she tried and tried to get a perfect run.

Her elbow was raw and bleeding. She had changed into her nightgown and her arms were so thin, the front hanging limply on one side where she'd lost a breast some years before. She was hunched over with the pain. I went into the bathroom, looking for some Neosporin and some gauze, but there wasn't any gauze and, because I had had some drinks and I was in a rush to go out to a party, I pulled some Icy Hot out of the medicine cabinet by mistake and went back to her bedroom and rubbed it all over my mother's wound.

She gave a small distant cry. "Oh. That hurts so much. It hurts." The tears were rolling down her cheeks. I ran to the bathroom and wet a washrag and went back and tried to wipe away the burning Icy Hot, but of course it was deep in the wound by then, and it wouldn't come out, and I was late for the party, and I finally said, "There. It'll be all right now." And I left her, I left her in burning pain, and I've never forgiven myself.

When my mother began really to die because the varices had come back, I was in a recording session in New York, making some fool commercial, some jingle. My sister called and told me about the anemia and the blood and I hung up the phone and said to everybody, "My mother's dying," and I got up and went home and called my friend Rocco, who was a doctor in Nashville. I described her symptoms, and asked him what was going to happen.

"Your mother will weaken because they won't be able to stop the blood. She won't get the best care because doctors don't try very hard with alcoholics because they know they'll just do it again. She'll start to lose her mind and dementia will set in, so if you want to have a rational conversation with her, you better go fast. And she'll be dead in ten days." I went down the next afternoon.

It was hot late August, almost Labor Day, and my mother was moved to a hospital in Roanoke, fifty miles away. Every morning I'd get up and drive my father to see her, and every afternoon I'd drive back and see her again about five o'clock. I don't remember what we talked about. They were giving her blood transfusions and she had come to look forward to them. "I hope they give me another one soon, because they make me feel so good." She was dying in a dream. Sometimes my sister would go with me and sometimes not.

I somehow thought there would be a moment of clarity, that she would open her eyes and say to me that all that had happened with her and me and my father was not my fault. I longed with all my heart for her to say that thing, but she never did.

I tried to prepare my family for what was going to happen, but my sister couldn't accept it out of her deep affection, and my father wouldn't accept it because it wouldn't cut through the haze and because I guess he really did love her; they were obsessed with each other, in a way. "No, no," he would say. "She'll have this little cancer episode and then she'll be home and we'll have another year."

The doctors had discovered that her breast cancer had returned, but they weren't going to give her chemo because it wasn't cancer that was killing her, but my family all pretended that was what was going on. My aunt, my mother's sister, whose heart was filled with grace and affection beyond reason, couldn't bear the thought of her sister in pain, or dying, especially dying of alcoholism. I called my brother every day and told him to come from Atlanta immediately, but he kept putting it off another day. Scenes of pain, and hospitals, made him anxious.

My mother's mind began to go. She became vague and unfocused; sometimes she didn't know who we were. Still, I drove an hour each way every morning and every night. On the morning of the ninth day, I drove my father down and let them sit for awhile and talk by themselves. She seemed fairly alert. She seemed better. She had gained some weight. As I took him out of the room, I promised her I would come back that afternoon to see her.

I lay by my sister's pool, and then it was time for me to go. "Don't go," she said. "You're so tired. It's a long way and you're tired." But I got up and got in the car and went home and changed my clothes to go to the hospital. I could hardly see for exhaustion.

I drove two miles out of town and pulled the car over to the side of the road. It was on a wooded incline near Buffalo Creek and you could feel the first cool breeze of the afternoon. I put my head on the steering wheel and decided to turn around, to go tomorrow when I took my father. But I knew there were some promises you don't break, so I picked my head up and drove on.

When I got to the hospital it was clear she was dying. She

had this delusion that she was rehearsing a play in London with Bruce Willis and she was late for rehearsal. She leaned forward, and her nightgown opened, and I could see the hollow where her breast had been, and a series of small nodules, a constellation, across her chest.

She had lost her mind, and her breathing came in shallow gasps, and I knew she was dying. I sat with her and held her hand and told her I would miss her; then I went to find the nurse and told her to call the doctor right away because my mother's condition was so grave. I used the word *grave*. And then I went back and kissed her and told her I loved her and I left. I don't know why I left her to die alone, but I did.

Yes. I went home to tell my father that my mother was going to die that night, and call my sister and call my brother, who finally said he would fly up the next day. My father went up to bed, and I slept on a foldout sofa in the dining room with the telephone by me on a little table, so I could answer it on the first ring and not wake my father. I lay awake all night and the phone rang at seven in the morning, a nurse calling to say that my mother had died. I told my father when he came downstairs and he went back up to bed and rarely left it for the next three days.

She was sixty-six years old.

My brother arrived and my sister and I picked him up as we were on the way to collect my mother's few things, a shabby, cheap overnight case, some pictures of her grandchildren. Her room so empty, the sheets already made up crisp and white. My brother was angry he had missed seeing her, although we all knew he would never have come, he would never have seen her in pain, never have visited her in a hospital to watch her die.

That afternoon, I took everybody's clothes to the dry cleaners so we would all look spruce, like we were the Kennedys or something. At least my father would look presentable.

We had to sit and talk with all the people who came. My father wouldn't come downstairs. The flowers and the roses and the bouquets were amazing. Many people wept as they sat with us, mostly her women friends. There was a blue slipper chair in the sitting room where my mother had always sat, and nobody would sit there.

It was in that chair that my mother said the most extraordinary thing. Years before. We were sitting with a couple, some friends of my parents, a doctor and his wife, when suddenly the wife, who was a wit, asked this question: If you were a character in literature, who would you be? Not who would you want to be, but who is it in literature you most closely resemble?

The doctor's wife said she was Elizabeth Bennet. And she really was. I don't remember what the doctor said. I said I was Rawdon Crawley, a lie in every way. My father said with remarkable self-awareness that he was Mr. Micawber. And then my mother spoke. "I'm the Lady Brett Ashley," she said.

"Why?" the doctor's wife asked.

"Because I believe in living the way she lived. You wreck your own life and then, very gently, you wreck the lives of those around you." Nobody knew what to say. She was sitting in the blue chair when she said this, and I never looked at it without remembering what she said. Now people wiped away tears when they imagined her sitting there again, so witty and pretty and chic, the way she had been before it all, or not before it all, but before it all got out of hand.

Her funeral was straightforward, after some trauma about the old prayer book versus the new prayer book, and my aunt and I went and took communion at three in the afternoon, before the service, just the two of us. It was lovely and comforting, in a small kind of way. At the funeral, we sang "For all the saints who from their labors rest" and "Come, labor on." Ora Labora. I still cry when I hear it. I hope they sing the same hymns at my funeral, and the Allegri Miserere.

People loved my mother very much. They surrounded her with affection and regard and it was never enough. People were so gentle with her, and waited for her bons mots. And she was kind and thoughtful and wrote a beautiful thank-you note.

In private, she was both vicious and adoring. She told me that, when I was born, I was such a beautiful baby that she wouldn't pick me up for a year. I'm not sure into which category that falls.

And I rubbed Icy Hot on her open wound.

The night after her funeral, my mother unburied, after everybody had left, we went over to my sister's for a swim and I got so drunk I had to be driven home and I fell down on the sidewalk. The next day my aunt, who wasn't there, said to me sadly, "Don't ever do that again."

But that night, after I went to bed, I woke up at two o'clock in the morning. I had not shed one tear for my mother the whole time she was sick or since her death. I went down to the kitchen and poured a glass of iced tea, and I started to cry. Not just cry, bawl. I cried so hard I was embarrassed, even alone, and I somehow thought that maybe it was the kitchen, so I took my iced tea into the next room and sat down exhausted in a chair and I started crying again. I moved through every room downstairs, drinking iced tea and crying for my mother. I sat in her blue slipper chair and felt the velvet and smelled her and cried. It was almost light when I went to bed.

I spent every night for the next six months in New York getting fucked up in every conceivable way. I would come home at one or two in the morning, so drunk and high on cocaine and fresh from some anonymous sexual encounter with somebody I wouldn't recognize on the street the next morning that I hardly knew where I was. Sometimes I couldn't pronounce my address for the cab driver. I got mugged five times on my own block. I did weird things like decide to make potato chips in the middle of the night, slicing the potatoes razor thin and dropping them one by one in sizzling oil in my disgusting kitchen in my disgusting apartment.

And one night I picked up a pack of cards and sat down on the floor with a bottle of Heineken and started playing solitaire. I played for hours. I finally crawled to my bed and passed out, but the next night, when I came home drunk, the cards were still there, and I played again. I played every night for weeks and I couldn't figure out why. It was just what I did. Then I remembered lying awake in my room at home in Virginia, before things got so out of control for me that I would sweat through my shirt walking five blocks to work, lying awake and listening to my mother playing solitaire. The Lady Brett whose work was done.

I played for months, until one night, I played a perfect game. All the cards fell into place, one after another. I didn't cheat. I just turned over the cards one by one, and one by one they turned out to be the right card, like a pitcher throwing a perfect game. And when it was done, when the cards were lying in four neat piles, every suit in order ace to king, I picked up the cards and put them in a drawer.

I never played solitaire again.

III

My aunt Dodo was severely retarded. She was not only retarded, she was deformed. Her left arm ended in a little nubby stump with a small red nipple on the end of it and she had a short, stumpy body and a large head and piercing eyes. People said she'd been retarded by scarlet fever at the age of two, but it looked to me like she had been retarded since day one. Apparently it never occurred to anybody that Dodo wasn't exactly an appropriate name for her. She was born Virginia, that was her real name, but she was called Dodo all her life. My grandfather, my father's father, was a drunk, the kind who wrecked cars and had to be sent away, and my father often had to go get him at the country club or wherever he was making a scene and help him home but, after Dodo's mind went blank, he never took a single drink again.

After his death, Dodo slept in my grandmother's bedroom until my grandmother died. They slept in twin beds. She would brush my grandmother's hair in the morning with a silver hairbrush that had soft, yellowed bristles.

Dodo's mental age was about four. She wore her hair in a little haircut kind of like Christopher Robin's, and she wore checked shirtwaist dresses with thin leather belts and saddle oxfords and short cotton socks. She could dress herself and even tie her own shoelaces, a feat which always stupefied us as children.

She smoked like a madwoman, and every morning at eleven, she and my grandmother would sit down and have a glass of sauterne. They would drink sauterne pretty much throughout the rest of the day, so that besides being short and thick and dressed like a child, Dodo was drunk most of the time.

My grandmother had a cook named Martha who came at six in the morning and left at eight at night, and she had Warren, a gentleman boarder who did a lot in the way of keeping things running smoothly. She would sit down every morning at the telephone table and order her groceries from the Jones Brothers, Bobby and Ogle, I swear, so she didn't have much to do except drink sauterne and nap and buy crabs from Archie Newton when he came by in the truck— softshells when they were in season— and big tins of potato chips from the Charles Chips man, who also came by in a truck once a week. She always looked lovely. She was known to be a great cook, but really all she ever did was sit in the enormous kitchen and tell Martha what to do, how to make deviled crab or angel food cake, recipes which Martha must have known by heart, after all those years.

Dodo watched television. Dodo was in love with the flickering image, and she would sit on the floor and watch anything that was on. She loved the early soap operas. She loved *American Bandstand.* She was a romantic.

She was the greatest playmate a child could have. She was strong, so when we played horsey she could carry an eight-year-old boy on her back with ease, crawling around the sitting room on all fours for hours, one eye on the TV. We would use her thin belts for reins. We would also arm wrestle and Dodo would always win. And, like all children, she could be mean, hurting you for no reason, pinching you until you bruised. But most of the time she was sweet and funny and amenable, and we adored her. My parents would pack us off to Fredericksburg in the summer so my grandmother could look after us, but she was old, and Warren was downtown working, and Dodo, except for nap time, was always available. Once my parents went to the Adirondacks, to Onteora, unimaginably far away, and we were at my grandmother Jinks's house for three weeks.

Jinks was extraordinarily mean to me. She was my father's mother, she doted on him, and she considered my brother and sister to be part of her family, since they were named after members of it, and I was considered to be part of my mother's family, since I was named after my mother's father. She would sit us all down, my brother and my sister and me, and she would say, "Look now, children. Everybody thinks Robbie's so smart, but we all know that he's just good at imitating the grownups. That's not really intelligence. A parrot can do that. You two are really the smart ones."

She would also sit me down with a family photograph album and show me pictures of one of my father's uncles who was also named Robbie. He looked like Rudolph Valentino, hair all slicked back, three-quarter profile in the World War I uniform, dark handsome eyes, completely handsome everything. "This is your uncle Robbie, whom you're named after," she would say, even though we both knew it wasn't true. "It's a pity you'll never be good-looking like he was."

I would spend days every summer in this house with this woman, living her life and trying not to feel too bad.

Breakfast was elaborate, served in several courses: a fruit course, and then big silver trays with scrambled eggs and bacon or ham or shad roe. There would always be fresh biscuits with country butter. My grandmother had a lifetime collection of elaborately painted teacups, and they gleamed from a china cupboard in the dining room.

Dinner was served in the middle of the day, and it was roast beef or roast chicken or a fresh fish or deviled crab with vegetables and rolls or more biscuits, followed by dessert, and all of this was made by Martha and served from her seat by my grandmother, who had taken up the duty after my grandfather's death and never relinquished it. Supper, after Martha left, after cocktails, was light, sandwiches or sliced chicken and, of course, potato chips. Dodo ate voraciously. She never seemed to run out of hunger. She was just hungry all the time.

Then we'd sit on the terrace in the warm summer night, drinking Cokes out of brightly colored aluminum glasses. The ice would melt in the glasses after five minutes. Cokes tasted different back then, better, or at least they seemed to have more fervor, on the terrace in the bright pink or ruby or turquoise glasses, in the dark with the humid smell of the caladium and mimosa. As we sat and moved slowly back and forth on a glider, the grownups had grease cutters, which is what some Virginia people call what normal people call nightcaps. They drank Tom Collinses from five o'clock until time to go to bed.

Dodo was in love with Frank Sinatra. She had seen him in movie magazines and then on the big screen. My grandmother took her, took us all, to grownup movies like *Advise and Consent*, scandalous movies with sex and violence, and Dodo had developed a passion for him in *From Here to Eternity* that was unstoppable. She believed that Frank would love her, too, and so she wrote to him nearly every day. She couldn't write, of course, but she had developed a scribble that resembled what her handwriting would look like if she could actually write. It was an elegant scrawl, broken in word-length bits, and divided into paragraphs, and started with what would have been "Dear Frank," except that it was just scribblescrabble. Gibberish.

She would write these letters, working at them for hours at the dining room table, and she would address an envelope in her scribble, and put a stamp on it, and ask Warren to mail it. He would pocket the letters and throw them away when he got to work. Every day she worked on her scrapbook filled with pictures of Frank Sinatra, and every day she asked if she'd gotten a letter from Frank, and the fact that she didn't never lessened her assurance or her affection for the star of her dreams.

She also wanted to go to Mary Washington College, so she wrote them letter after letter, but they never answered either. It mystified her and eventually enraged her that they wouldn't let her enroll. There was a building there named after her uncle.

So Warren, one day, sat down at the office and wrote her a reply. He carefully copied the style of her gibberish, wrote her a long letter, and put it in an envelope and addressed it in scribblescrabble and put a stamp on it. He brought it home that night, and proudly told Dodo that the letter from Mary Washington had finally come.

She looked at the envelope suspiciously, opened the letter,

and said, "This is just scribblescrabble," and started crying. She was inconsolable for days, and she never wrote to Mary Washington again, appalled that they would play such a foolish game with her.

She also read the funnies every day. She couldn't read, of course, but she would look at the pictures and make up elaborate stories about Judge Parker or Steve Canyon and Poteet, who was always getting caught in Communist concentration camps where rats crawled all over her and the women wore skintight leather fetish outfits. We would sit at her feet and howl. Sometimes we were laughing with her, but a lot of the time we were laughing at her.

When I was fourteen, my grandmother died. She was old and she just died, in a nursing home she loathed. The night of her funeral, the grownups all went to the country club for dinner, and I was left to babysit for the children, which included Dodo. We ate sandwiches at my aunt's house while Dodo drank sauterne, and then we all watched Ernie Kovacs or somebody on television, and then I put the little ones to bed while Dodo smoked and drank and stared at the TV.

Later, when Dodo was going to the bathroom, I sneaked a cigarette out of her pack. I told her I was going to sit outside for awhile, and I sat on the steps of the back porch and smoked a menthol cigarette. Just as I was finishing, Dodo came out on the porch and I flicked the cigarette into the hard, spiky grass that grows there.

I was afraid she would catch me smoking and tell my parents. But she didn't say a word.

Dodo sat down next to me and pulled her cigarettes out of

her pocket and lit one with the little lighter she could operate with one hand. She smoked with a voluptuousness and an ecstasy that was very glamorous, savoring every puff as though it were good champagne, rolling the smoke around in her mouth, then sucking it deep into her lungs and exhaling with a long, smooth sigh through her mouth and her nose.

Then we just sat in silence, looking at the stars. She smelled like Yardley Lavender, as my grandmother always had, and she was as familiar to me as dirt and it was nice.

Then Dodo moved a little closer to me. Then she moved a little closer. Our hips were touching. She laid her left arm casually across my thin shoulders, and we sat and looked at the stars. It was starting to turn creepy. Dodo said softly, still looking at the stars, "Kiss me." I turned and kissed her on the cheek.

Suddenly her strong deformed arm tightened on my shoulders and I was pulled toward her, into her breasts, into the sweat and the lavender and the musk of this child, and she whispered softly in my ear even as her arm tightened in an unbreakable grip, "No. I mean *really* kiss me." Like in the movies. The way Frank kissed Ava. The way grownups kissed in the parking lot at the country club.

I writhed out of her grasp and went inside, leaving her alone on the porch. When she came in the house, some minutes later, she didn't mention it, we just sat and watched television until my parents and aunt and uncle came home. I never told anyone.

I almost never saw Dodo again. She went to live with my aunt, who used Dodo's inheritance to put an addition on her house, an upstairs, so Dodo would have someplace to live.

My aunt made her stop drinking—that was hard—and then

she made her stop smoking—which was harder. I guess Dodo went on loving Frank Sinatra, or fell in love with somebody new like Hoss Cartwright, but I don't remember ever seeing her again. Not after the night when she so badly wanted me to kiss her.

She lived for a long time. I don't know how long—I never knew how old Dodo was—and I lost track, but it was after my mother died and before my father died that Dodo herself died.

My father was too worn down to go to the funeral, and my sister had a sick child, and my brother, well, he lived in Atlanta, and I felt it was only right that somebody from my side of the family go down there and go to her funeral.

I took the shuttle to National and rented a car. Tom Brokaw was standing in front of me in line. I showed up at my aunt's an hour before the funeral. It was cold, late winter, and I was wearing a black cashmere overcoat, trying to look happy and successful, but my aunt took one look at me and said disapprovingly, "You've put on weight." Gaining weight in my family was as startling and reprehensible as murder in the general population. Her house was filled with silver and pictures and the painted teacups, all from my grandmother's house, in some rooms practically floor to ceiling. We sat around, drinking sherry, waiting for the time to go to the cemetery.

Then we drove down there, to this cemetery where Dodo was to be buried, filled with Civil War generals and some of the best families, the most distinguished in the state. It's a state where that kind of thing matters. It had rained in the night, a downpour, and the rain had caused Dodo's grave to cave in, so where there was supposed to be a crisp hole there was only sludge. Her coffin was set up on a bier in the middle of the cemetery, beneath a marquee. The undertaker took one look at my black overcoat and my black scarf and suit, and concluded immediately that I must be a rival undertaker, come to steal away his business. He finally asked Warren, who told him I was the dead woman's nephew.

Tom Faulkner had stepped out of retirement to do the ceremony. He had been a minister to my family for a long time, and had done our weddings and funerals and christenings since Jesus was a baby. He must have been eighty, but he looked pretty spruce in his cassock and cotta, standing there rosy-cheeked in the cold.

Dodo's coffin was not small. She must have been in her fifties, her child's lank hair would have been entirely gray by now, and she must have weighed more than two hundred pounds. We gathered under the awning that was near Dodo's collapsed grave, and Tom Faulkner began to speak, with infinite kindness and affection, and I realized that he was reading the service that's for the burial of a child. I had never heard it before. It's at the very end of the old prayer book, just before the Psalms, and every word was new to me.

"Verily I say unto you, Except ye be converted, and become as little children, ye shall not enter into the kingdom of heaven. And whoso shall receive one such little child in my name receiveth me. Take heed that ye despise not one of these little ones; for I say unto you, That in heaven their angels do always behold the face of my Father which is in heaven."

And "Grant us steadfastly to believe that this thy child hath been taken into the safekeeping of thine eternal love; through Jesus Christ our Lord. Amen."

Then the prayer book goes on: "When they are come to the Grave shall be said or sung, 'Jesus saith to his disciples, Ye now therefore have sorrow: but I will see you again, and your heart shall rejoice, and your joy no man taketh from you.'

"While the earth is being cast upon the Body, the Minister shall say, 'In sure and certain hope of the Resurrection to eternal life through our Lord Jesus Christ, we commit the body of this child to the ground. The Lord bless Virginia and keep her, the Lord make his face to shine upon her and be gracious unto her, the Lord lift up his countenance upon her, and give her peace, both now and evermore.'"

It's the only time I ever cried at a funeral, except at my aunt Anne's when they sang "For All the Ships at Sea," such an odd choice for a landlocked county in western Virginia. She loved it for some reason; she had had it sung at her wedding, too.

But Tom Faulkner had called Dodo Virginia, while still acknowledging that she was no more than a child, never had been.

"O God, whose most dear Son did take little children into his arms and bless them; Give us grace, we beseech thee, to entrust the soul of this child to thy neverfailing care and love, and bring us all to thy heavenly kingdom; through the same thy Son, Jesus Christ our Lord. Amen."

And after a short blessing to comfort the living, it was over. It had taken maybe twelve minutes, after coming all that way, but, as we filed out, past the mess of what was supposed to be Dodo's grave, at that moment, I wished everybody in the world could be part of my family: the kindness and the graciousness, my aunt and uncle's infinite good humor; the way my grandmother Jinks had made it all run so smoothly on no money at all, she had once bought a mink coat and was offended when the store called to ask for payment three years later; the way the heat would settle on the awnings in the summer nights and everybody would sit outside on the terrace until long after dark; the way Warren had once helped us plant a piece of bubblegum at the bottom of a little willow tree and, in the morning, we had gotten up to find the whole tree covered with pieces of Bazooka; the way he would take us for the world's best limeades at the Rexall, made from real, fresh limes, and let us steer the car on the long bridge home; the way my aunt could dive from a dock into the Potomac in a perfectly graceful arc, her long legs tanned, her body slim as a boy's; the way the women in the family wore bathing caps and little rubber shoes when they went in the river; the way we would ride our bicycles down the lane and across to a creek where an ex-prizefighter called Bar' Foot Green cooked crabs over an eternal fire of burning tires; the way we ate tomato sandwiches with the edges cut off, sometimes for days on end in the hot summers, even the way we said *tomato;* the way my grandmother could pick a crab completely clean with her needlelike fingers, her two huge diamonds flashing in the ring on her hand; my mother sitting in her blue slipper chair, my father sipping his drink and telling a story about his old friend Sam, who took a live turkey with him to Thanksgiving dinner in a roadhouse because he felt so guilty about the mass slaughter of the turkey's brethren; the way people dressed up, back then, in evening dresses and tuxedos and linen suits and white dinner jackets for dinner at the club; the way Martha never complained, even though she stayed in that hot kitchen all day and went to the bathroom in an outhouse out back, in the yard, in a little hut I had always thought was a toolshed; the way we bore grief with dignity and grace; the way things never changed, even though everything had changed around us and nothing had turned out the way people imagined it would and we weren't successful or rich and some of us were tragically and disastrously unhappy and many of us were already dead, too young, and I had tried to kill myself six years before, one of my dark secrets, blue razor and blue ruin, on the night of my thirty-fifth birthday, the fat scars still purple on my arms beneath my excellent clothes, while Dodo had lived a life with no more trouble than the fact that Frank Sinatra never answered her letters; the way she was buried as a child. I wanted, at that moment, for things to have stayed the way they were forever. I wanted, at that moment, for everybody to be us, and for us to be whole and clean and shining, the way we had meant to be. I wanted Dodo to go home to Jesus and be slim and tall and whole and happy and smart and loved by movie stars.

"Kiss me," she had said in the dark. It was already almost thirty years ago. "No. Really kiss me." Like in the movies. The way Frank kissed Ava Gardner.

Maybe I'm Amazed

My brother's head blew up. This had nothing to do with dropping the big flat rock on his skull. That was a game. That was a long time before. That was when we were boys, when we would stand by the creek and see who could pick up the biggest rock and raise it over his head and toss it in the creek. My brother was two years older than I was, and athletic, and he almost always won. Every game, practically, ended with the winner dropping a large flat stone on the top of his head, while my sister watched laughing with her little girlfriends, and a great deal of blood ensued, and howling and usually stitches. During the dinner hour. Imagine.

Once, blood streaming from my brother's head, we walked into the middle of an outdoor cocktail party, on the green back terrace, little trays of cucumber sandwiches sweating on the wrought iron Salterini filigree cocktail table, the men in shorts, some of them, all of them in those shirts that men with big forearms wear. One of the guests, a doctor on his third or fourth Highball, was called upon to examine him. "Hell," he said, "the damned hole's no bigger than a quarter." Everybody laughed. This same doctor was given to singing only the first line of a remarkably irritating song, "She's got trains, bells, and whistles in her ears." After which, with a pumping gesture of his noncock-tail hand, he would scream in a falsetto, "Whooo! Whooo!" Everybody thought this was very funny. People laughed until they wept, even after the twentieth or fiftieth time.

The blood matted my brother's hair to his scalp. We were so used to it; it was, almost, the whole point of the game, and he wasn't even crying. We just went upstairs to my grandmother Miss Nell, who had been a nurse, and she applied penicillin ointment and a bandage. She always said not to use penicillin ointment too often, because you'd get immune to it, but she always used it anyway.

My grandmother Miss Nell was sweet and benign and incredibly forthright. We lived in her house. She was both strong and kind and she was a widow for thirty-five years and served herself breakfast in bed every morning, going down to the kitchen and making strong coffee and cereal with cream so thick you could stand a spoon up in it, and sausages or grits. Then she would carry the whole thing up to her bedroom on a breakfast tray, and eat in her lonely bed all by herself, and I loved her with all my heart and I still think of her every day. She had a way of addressing you as "baby" which was not at all like a Holly-wood mogul but that was wholly sweet and endearing, like a mother with an infant, or rather a small child, and I can hear it in my head to this day and I couldn't imitate it in a million years. I've tried.

I still live in her house. I always hope she would like the way it looks now, but I fear she'd find it tricked out and pretentious, although most people seem to like it fine. Miss Nell. My mother's mother. Not the other one.

My brother's head blowing up had nothing to do with any of that. My grandmother was already dead by then. He was thirty-five; about the age, actually, that most people's heads blow up, if they're going to. Senator Joseph Biden's head blew up the same year. So did Quincy Jones's. They went right on being senators and winning Grammys.

My brother was at a Saturday night cocktail party in Atlanta, where he was spending his days being a brilliant reporter for the *Wall Street Journal,* although he knew nothing about economics, as far as I could tell, not one soul in the family did, when all of a sudden he got a splitting headache. His wife and a nurse who was present concluded that he was having a migraine. He'd never had one before, but both of them had, and he did have all the symptoms of a migraine—the speckles in his vision, the searing pain on one side of his head—and one of them was a nurse, after all, a nurse and a migraine sufferer, and it all seemed logical.

He went home to dark rooms and cold compresses and vomiting and all of the rest of it. He stayed in bed all day Sunday, watching sports and dozing and putting up with this incredible pain and nothing changed, still the same relentless blinding agony.

On Monday morning he woke up, the pain just the same, and his wife said to go make some coffee, to move around a little bit to see how he felt. He got up and walked across the room. He bent over and picked up his shoe.

"What is this?" he asked.

"It's your shoe," his wife said.

"I know that," he said. "I know that. But what do you do with it?"

In half an hour he was at DeKalb General, having a CAT scan. He had a berry aneurysm, a congenital weakness of one of the blood vessels in his brain, and it had started oozing blood on Saturday night. If it burst, he would have a cerebral hemorrhage and die. If it didn't, they could operate, and put a little clamp on it, and he could go on with his life. Like Joseph Biden did. Like Quincy Jones.

When your blood vessels start oozing blood into the brain, the brain swells, and when you operate on the brain, your brain swells some more, so he had to lie flat on his back, not moving, for ten days, while various drugs were pumped into him to make the swelling go down before they could operate. Too much swelling, and no oxygen gets into the brain, causing brain damage.

I flew down there right away, and it was just a horrible situation. His wife, who hated me, was eight months pregnant, and her family, who were grim, sour-faced, hard-line Southern Methodists, except for her sister-in-law Judy Judy, who may have been a Methodist but in no way could be called hard-line, were sitting around the waiting room as though the funeral were about to take place any minute, and it was pretty hardcore. His wife was a wreck, so much so that she sort of forgot for a minute that she hated me with every fiber of her being. Just for a minute.

She was one of those small-town Southern girls who are raised to believe that they are just the prettiest, smartest, best little things on the face of the earth, and sometimes they are. She was from a town called Social Circle, Georgia. She might as well have owned Social Circle, Georgia, in its entirety.

So, what with the black dresses and the aroma of bar soap and the pregnancy and the general air of entitlement, it was pretty ghastly. My brother lying on a hospital bed with his head in restraints covered in lamb's wool like a taxicab driver's car seat seemed almost too abstract to take in. It was too horrible. He was my older brother and he was my beloved. Not to mention it runs in families, and siblings are far more likely to have the same thing happen to them. I did not want the same thing to happen to me, particularly not in Atlanta, at DeKalb General Hospital.

My sister-in-law, even though she has turned out to be a much finer person as the years have passed, loyal and good-humored and capable of acts of great kindness, hated me so much that she'd actually told me how much she hated me. She was a holy terror in those days. She had come to New York, before she and my brother were married, and she had stayed with me in my disgusting apartment on Thirty-fifth Street. One night, I had taken her out to a restaurant in Chinatown and, looking at me over green tea, she had actually said it: "I hate you. I've always hated you, and I'll hate you until the day you die. I hate your guts, and there's not a thing you can do about it." And I actually paid for dinner. A doormat, my mother had once said to me.

We then went back to my grotty apartment, where she proceeded, in the night, to come down with the flu, so she lay in my bed for four days while I slept on the sectional aqua sofa left over from the previous tenants, who were waiters at the Westchester Country Club and who had left everything behind and did not own one thing that was not in bad taste, and I took care of her. Fed her chicken soup and listened to her vomit. Jeez. That kind of loathing.

It was all because of another trip to New York, when she had gone to bed early and my brother and I had sat up real late drinking Jack Daniels and discussing our internal affairs, and I had finally told him it was time he did something with his life. He had been a classic slacker. Actually he had had a kind of Episcopalian nervous breakdown and been thrown out of Williams, where once, when I was visiting, I discovered that he hadn't opened a letter in six months. So he'd been booted and drafted into the army, where he served for three years in this dreary little town in Germany. It had one distinguishing feature: It had an organ once played by Mozart. I went there to visit him because my parents hadn't heard from him for months and I was living in Torremolinos, Spain, and they figured it was an easy hop to go over and check up on him, which I did, walking for hours the dismal streets of this dismal town, waiting for my brother to get off duty so I could meet him in a tacky discotheque and watch him get drunk and stoned. I learned the only German word I know, *kellerfensterhalter,* which means a little thing that holds a cellar window open, and I kept thinking: These people were all Nazis.

So years later, in my apartment in New York, we were discussing, over the many glasses of Jack Daniels, his general lack of direction, and I had happened to mention that it was time he did something with his life. I told him I'd already been working for three years and he was two years older than I was and I was tired of being the younger brother and the older brother at the same time and I told him I thought he'd make a terrific journalist.

"I'd never do that," he said. "It would sully my soul." He actually said that. Sully my soul. He's the only person I've ever heard use the word *sully* in conversation.

It turned out his future wife was listening to all this, and she had somehow conceived the notion that I was being unbearably cruel to my brother, and I actually think he had won her heart by telling her all the heartbreaking stories of the various cruelties he had suffered at our hands, his own family—the neglect, the slights, the missing the Little League games because they all came at cocktail hour when nobody was allowed to do anything—my darling, unique brother whom I adored, as I have said, but who really did need to do something with his life. And who actually did go to journalism school, where he wrote his graduate thesis on a punk rock music club, and go on to be a brilliant young journalist in Atlanta, which is where he was when his head blew up.

But she had heard the conversation and her mind was made up. She hated me. It didn't seem likely to change, tragedy or not.

He lay there so helpless and quiet and afraid and every part of his body was soft. His upper arms were unbearably white. His wife was getting massive amounts of attention and he seemed so alone, so unattended, although he wasn't; it's just that when you're so close to death, there's no amount of attention that's going to assuage the calamity, at least no amount or kind a normal person could give.

I slept in the guest room in their townhouse apartment thing, whatever those things are, and I drove his car back and forth to the hospital all the time. It was a nifty little convertible, an Alfa Romeo or something, and I loved that car. His wife slept on a cot in the hospital, surrounded by Methodists, and she wept a lot, which is understandable. The hard part was trying to give any real comfort to somebody who so clearly despised me.

The ten days passed in a languid agony. I shopped for food. I did the laundry. I took my brother's wife into the chapel and read poetry to her. She only wanted to hear poems about death. She said that, if he died, she would wait to have the baby and then kill herself. She was very young, not even thirty.

My parents flew down to Atlanta for the operation, these people who never went anywhere, except to Nags Head for three weeks every summer. My sister and her husband came down, leaving my five-year-old niece at home with their friends Teddy and his wife. My sister and her husband stayed with Judy Judy and her husband, but still it was pretty tight quarters in the townhouse with my mother and father since nobody wanted to sleep in my brother's bed, and so I ended up on the sofa again.

I made dinner for everybody, a cold tenderloin of beef. It was Memorial Day weekend. I asked my sister-in-law's best friend whether the piece of meat was big enough.

"How much did you pay for it?" she asked.

"Thirty-five dollars."

"That's enough."

My parents were out of their element, and very afraid, and they seemed frail. They were very brave, I thought. Brave, and they were besotted with my brother, even after he wrecked his brand-new car in Germany and took it to the repair shop to have the axle replaced and never went back to pick it up so my father had to buy a car he never saw because he had cosigned for it or something. It was just the abstract of an automobile somewhere in Kaiserslautern, Germany.

They adored him enough to leave home. Even when my sister was broke and alone with a two-year-old baby and she got tularemia from Bubba, her rabbit, that summer everybody got Legionnaires' Disease, they wouldn't go up to Martha's Vineyard to see her.

They brought along their own bourbon, in their Samsonite suitcases, as though, in all of Atlanta, you couldn't buy an inexpensive but drinkable bottle of bourbon. They did that all the time. They took bourbon to the beach. They brought their own bourbon to London, when they came to visit me there, although that made a lot more sense. My mother in her nightgown reminded me of my brother, all underbelly. Pale and slack, without muscle, soft and vulnerable.

The night before the operation, when the swelling in my brother's brain had finally gone down enough, Judy Judy had the whole mismatched family to dinner. The Methodists didn't drink, of course; my parents did. Here's what Judy Judy had: a casserole that was made with skinless chicken breasts on the bottom, then a layer of canned asparagus, then a sauce of cream of mushroom soup, the whole thing covered with a layer of corn flakes. I had been to Lutece. I had been to Grenouille. I was sure it would be revolting. I was wrong. It was absolutely delicious. I was ravenous. I couldn't get enough of it.

Judy Judy, who was later to go crazy in her own particular way, imagining a ravaging breast and/or cervical cancer she didn't actually have, even going around the country giving brave lectures about living with a deadly cancer, driving her perfectly ordinary, nice husband to fall to pieces and hate her and, finally, to leave her, was then a blond, amusing woman with enormous breasts who adored butterflies. She was covered in butterfly jewelry, some costume and some real; all the magnets on her refrigerator were butterflies; the paper napkins had butterflies on them. The plates had butterflies on them. The sofas and chairs were covered with needlepoint butterfly pillows. In the bathroom, the toilet paper was covered with little butterflies. I'm not kidding. Aunt Minnie Lee Lee, who before I met her I had assumed was Chinese but who in reality had married silent Mr. Lee twice, said she thought Judy Judy and the butterfly thing were strange, although she was just being conversational. For a Methodist, she was not afraid to express her opinions.

Aunt Minnie Lee Lee had the habit of saying, whenever anything had pleased her particularly, or even when she just felt like being cordial, "Well, now, my, that was a refrasher." She thought Judy Judy's chicken casserole was a real refrasher.

But nobody in the South ever thinks that anything done by a family member is really strange, or rather, their strange deeds are merely more endearing. Judy Judy called everybody *dawlin'* as though she really meant it, and she probably did, and she just said the butterfly was her personal symbol. It gave her hope.

As dinner parties on the night before your brother's brain operation go, it was a huge success. My parents had their bourbon. The teetotalers had their soft drinks and iced tea. Judy Judy had her butterflies. Everybody got along. The chicken casserole gave cornflakes a whole new and magical aspect. We knew that tragedy had struck. We couldn't escape the image of my sedated brother lying over there at DeKalb General in head restraints. You don't forget that kind of thing just because the chicken casserole was yummy and nobody screamed at anybody else about religious issues and burning in hell for drinking bourbon whiskey. We knew that by the next night it could all be better or it could get a lot worse and there was the camaraderie of the terrified to hold us together. I was so afraid.

The operation was on Memorial Day. It was decided, since the hospital was less than a mile away, and because waiting in the waiting room with the Methodists was so grim, that my family would wait it out at my brother's place, where they could smoke and have access to the bourbon. I drove to the hospital early in the morning, the warm early summer breeze blowing through the Alfa. I had the top down, feeling smart. In the parking lot, I saw his surgeon's stainless steel gull-wing DeLorean. Brain surgeons think they're God. So did DeLorean. I once saw him try to cut in line at the movies in New York, only to be shouted down by the angry crowd. It seems sort of quaint now, waiting in line for a movie. Kind of sweet.

My function was to run back and forth all day, carrying news from the hospital to my family. At the hospital, the surgeon came out and told me and my brother's wife that the operation should take about three hours. It took eight and a half. It was a disaster. I guess he wasn't God after all.

The brain doesn't feel any pain. Getting through the skull hurts, although my brother was out, but once in the brain, the brain tissue itself doesn't feel pain.

As soon as they bored the hole and got into his brain, the aneurysm burst open, and he began hemorrhaging massive amounts of blood. The aneurysm was right at the base of his skull, where the artery divided, carrying blood to the left and right side of his brain.

It was interminable. The Methodists were mute or locked in silent prayer. My sister-in-law was distraught, so we sat in the chapel, reading more poems about dead people. We knew nothing about what was going on, only that it was going on for a very long time.

I ran back and forth to my family, six or seven times, carrying the no news there was, and they just waited. My sister made lunch for everybody: cold roast beef sandwiches that went uneaten.

When it was finally over, the surgeon came out and told us matter-of-factly that my brother had lost such massive amounts of blood that he was going to die. He was going to die in the night, before the sun came up. His brain was ruined, and he was going to die in the night. My sister-in-law behaved better than I thought she might, although she was, of course, inconsolable and talked about suicide again. I drove back to my parents to report the news. They had broken out the bourbon by that time and they were deeply, deeply moved. Stricken, as though by a snakebite. I then drove back to the hospital, where the surgeon came out again and told us that my brother had made a miraculous recovery in the last half hour, and that he would live, but he would be brain damaged and he was paralyzed on his left side and he was in a deep coma. There was no way of knowing how deeply his brain was damaged, or what form the damage would take.

The brain is a funny thing. If you're right-handed, they know where everything is—short-term memory, long-term memory, anger, patience—everything. There's even a microscopic pin-point area that is your personality, and they know where that is.

If you're left-handed, they don't know anything, the surgeon explained. It's all helter skelter, so if you lose a lot of blood, and your brain is certainly damaged, there's no way to tell what functions of the brain will be affected. My brother is left-handed.

My sister-in-law behaved pretty well about all this, and she retired into the arms of her family, and I drove back to the town-house to tell my family the change in prognosis, and they sort of collapsed in grief and joy; having prepared themselves for his death, they weren't quite sure how to deal with his prospects for a limited life.

Then I went back to the hospital, where the gull-wing surgeon spoke to us one more time and told us my brother was resting in the recovery room and then he would be moved to the ICU, while we waited for the swelling in his brain to go down.

I fed everybody dinner, and then my sister and brother-in-law went back to Judy Judy's to collapse. By ten o'clock, my sister-in-law asleep on her cot at the hospital, the stiff-backed Methodists gone home to their cold suppers, I managed to get my parents to bed, and then I sat down on the sitting room floor to have a drink and watch the news. I was exhausted, tired from the driving and the caretaking and the awfulness of the day in general. I was immediately drunk on one drink. I was so tired of taking care of everybody. I was so tired of being positive and polite to gull-wing and polite to my sister-in-law. While the news was going on I started crying. I cried so hard the tears shot out and ran down the inside of my glasses.

Then the phone rang. It was the husband of the couple who were taking care of my niece. His name was Teddy. Every man in the South is named after a four-year-old boy long dead. They have names like Zeke or Skip or Topher, as though leaving the frat house was the end of life's possibilities. He said he needed to speak to my brother-in-law. It was urgent. It was an emergency, he said.

I answered that if anything was wrong with my niece, if something had happened to her, he should tell me, and I would relay the news to my brother-in-law and my sister. They were staying somewhere else, I explained, as though that mattered.

"No, no," Teddy said. "It's nothing like that. She's fine. It's just that, well, their house burned down."

"What?" I said.

"Their house burned down. Some kids broke in and set it on fire and it burned down."

I started laughing hysterically. I couldn't help it. It was like something out of a Gothic story and it seemed so unreal it was comical. I leaned against the refrigerator and laughed until tears ran down my cheeks.

"No," said Teddy. "Maybe you're not getting it. Their house burned down."

"I got it," I said. "It's terrible. A terrible terrible tragedy. I'll tell them."

Suddenly my mother appeared on the stairs. She was wearing a flimsy blue nightgown and I could see her thin arms. She was so afraid she sat down on the steps and gripped the banister with her hand. I couldn't stop laughing.

"Their house burned down," I choked out, still roaring with laughter. "Somebody broke in. It burned up."

"What? What?" She kept saying. She was both drunk and exhausted from anguish. She had thought it was a call from the hospital saying my brother had died. She couldn't take the change in direction.

"He's fine," I said. "It wasn't the hospital. It was Teddy. Their house burned down." I was gasping with laughter. My mother slumped against the banister, like a child waiting for Christmas morning. I thought she was going to faint. I led her back to bed, where my father was snoring and gritting his teeth. He could make the most remarkable noises. He also talked in his sleep. I remember one night, after we had gotten back from two weeks at the beach, I woke up to hear them talking in their bed.

"I do everything for you," he said. "I buy you things. I take you for a nice vacation at the beach. The Golden Strand. What do I get? Not a word of thanks."

"Buy me things?" my mother said. "All you ever bought me was a goddamned Coke and a pack of Nabs." Our Nash Rambler always broke down with some terrible ailment, usually the generator, on the way to the beach, and one time we waited so long in this woebegone gas station in Coinjock that the gas station owner's wife took us into the back where they lived and made us sandwiches. But it was true we drank a lot of Cokes and ate a lot of Nabs in those gas stations.

I crept into their room. They were both totally asleep, facing away from each other. The next morning, neither one had the slightest recollection of the conversation.

When my mother was asleep again, I went to call my sister.

I pulled myself together enough to dial Judy Judy's number with a sense of serious purpose, even tragedy. As soon as I got my brother-in-law on the line, I started to tell him the news, but I started laughing and I couldn't stop. He finally got it, and he said, "Well, as long as your brother's OK, the rest doesn't matter. It's just stuff." Although I had known him all my life, I was struck with admiration, and my heart filled with love for him, for the first time since he had married my sister. He had a child's name, too.

I drank Tanqueray out of the bottle until my nerves turned to jelly and I hardly knew my own name, not that I thought of trying to think of my own name, and I laughed and cried in the night and I finally went to sleep on the sofa.

The next day, my sister and brother-in-law, in shock, went to the ICU to see my comatose brother for two minutes, which was all they were allowed, and then they came over before they started to drive back home. My sister said the most extraordinary thing. She suddenly looked up and said, "Gosh, all week I've missed my soaps."

"This *is* a soap opera," I said.

Then they got in the car and drove home, to start picking through their ruined things. They never caught the boys who did it.

The swelling in my brother's head didn't go down. They were afraid that the swelling would cut off the blood supply to his brain, leaving him a vegetable. So the surgeon came back and operated again. He patiently explained to my sister-in-law and me that he was going to go in and remove small parts of the frontal lobes of my brother's brain so it would have room to swell and not cut off the oxygen.

"He's having a frontal lobotomy," said my mother. "He'll be a zombie." I guess she was right, as I understand the term, although it didn't turn him into a zombie.

The operation took place, the surgeon said it was successful, and my brother went back to intensive care. He was still in a coma. He was still paralyzed, and there was an empty space in the front of his skull where part of his brain used to be.

The intensive care unit was an awful place, filled with little cubicles in which these horribly sick and wounded people lay, mostly waiting to die. We were allowed in twice a day for fifteen minutes.

There was this one guy who had had the most unusual accident imaginable. His name was Eric. He looked like Elvis Presley, just a Georgia redneck, but as handsome as a Greek god, black hair and blue cheeks and a finely chiseled nineteen-year-old face, and we had to pass him every time we went in to see my brother. He had been riding his motorcycle and he had lost control and run into a light pole and the gas tank of his bike had gone up his rectum and then it had exploded in flames. He sort of won the sweepstakes for the weirdest accident. There was a tent over his middle section, and all his organs, his vital organs, were hanging in little bags off the side of his bed. His face was totally calm and composed, not slack, just sleeping and handsome. You figured there was no way this guy was going to live, what with his liver and kidneys dangling in baggies off the metal rails of his bed, and he had nineteen operations, but somehow he lived through it.

His family waited in the waiting room with all the grim
Methodists, even a minister came to wait and pray, and they
were all beautiful. His fiancée looked like a runway model. Like
a biker's wet dream.

Then we just waited while my brother did nothing. I took my
mother swimming at a rich friend's mother's house. We drove out
to Buckhead, to West Paces Ferry Road, in the Alfa Romeo. It
was really hot, and it was barely summer. It was the kind of pool
that only really, really rich people have, with flowers and vines and
a changing house and falling water and nothing turquoise or vul-
gar about it anyplace. I swam, while my mother sat on the edge of
the pool with her legs in the water. She was the kind of woman,
even in her late fifties, who looked very good in a one-piece
bathing suit. She always said she only went in the water once a
year, at Nags Head. She wore a bathing cap when she went in. But
being there on West Paces Ferry Road seemed to make her feel
better, and I loved swimming in a rich woman's pool.

My parents came to see my brother before they flew back
home. My mother put a cross around my brother's neck and
kissed his hand. My brother suddenly said, without opening his
eyes, his right hand fingering the cross, "I want to see Stevie
Wonder. I have something to tell Stevie Wonder." Then he
lapsed back into silence.

People who are in comas don't look like they're sleeping
peacefully. They look inert. They look like a breathing dead person. Everything has gone slack. Whatever self they have has left
their bodies. We thought it a hopeful sign that he had said anything, that he had moved his hand.

Every day the motorcycle guy had another operation, and

there was one less baggy hanging off the side of his bed. Sometimes he was even conscious. They wouldn't even put him on
painkillers. He was so close to death they thought sedation
would put him over the edge. I don't know how he stood it. The
pain must have been terrible, what with the gas tank up the rectum and all.

My parents left. There was only so much trauma they could
stand, and they'd run out of their bourbon and my brother had
moved his hand and talked about Stevie Wonder and so they
left. My sister-in-law had taken to coming home for dinner, although she still slept at the hospital. I did her laundry. I cleaned
her toilets. I had people over for dinner I thought might comfort her. I had the woman who had said she gauged how much
meat to get by the price and not by the number of guests. My
sister-in-law was enormously pregnant.

We took turns going to the ICU. We could only go for fifteen
minutes twice a day, even though Elvis seemed to be surrounded
by fans and fellow bikers all the time. My sister-in-law would go
in the mornings, sometimes we would both go, sometimes I
would go and she would rest after a dinner I had cooked, surrounded by friends, and she would wait for news.

People in comas are not attractive. They have foul breath and
yellow cheese between their teeth and they stink. The motorcycle guy was not in a coma, he was just in unimaginable pain,
so his lights were sort of always out, but he was gorgeous every
time you looked at him. I think his family combed his Elvis hair,
black and shiny and pompadoured. My brother, with a cross
around his neck, a cheap cross, not even real silver, did not look
like somebody your heart cried out to see.

One night I went alone to see him, while my sister-in-law sat with her best friends at the dinner table. I walked in and started talking to him. I had taken to having these conversations with him, even though there was no indication that he would respond. I told him things that I thought would irritate him, to try to get a rise out of him. I told him our sister's house had burned down. I told him I had wrecked his car. I told him his wife had told me she would hate me forever.

This night, I talked about his stereo. My brother had a new stereo of which he was inordinately proud. We had talked about it on the phone, before his aneurysm, and I knew it meant a lot to him. He didn't want anybody to touch it. I knew he valued his record collection like gold, and I had noticed that, before his head blew up at the party, he had bought the new Paul McCartney album, the one with the cherries on the cover. So I told him I had played the McCartney album on his new stereo, and I had scratched the vinyl on both sides of the album. I was holding his thin right hand, and I told him I'd wrecked his new record.

He opened his eyes, and looked at me. "I know this is hard," he said. "I know you take care of everybody, but I want you to take care of yourself. I know it's been hard on you."

Then he closed his eyes, and he sang in a thin, whispery voice, so softly I could barely hear him, "Maybe I'm amazed at the way you're with me all the time. And maybe I'm amazed at the way I love you."

Then he lapsed back into a coma. But I knew he was going to live.

For the next three weeks, I flew down to Atlanta every weekend. I would leave on Thursday night after work, and come back on Sunday or Monday. They were very understanding at work, although, come to think of it, they fired me six months later, so maybe their patience was more superficial than it seemed.

I flew Delta F class, saying to myself I was so exhausted, and that was partially true, but also because you could get a lot of free drinks in first, without having to wait for the cart and then feeling guilty when you ordered a double gin and tonic, which was never enough anyway.

One time, I got so drunk on the plane that I went straight from the airport to a restaurant to meet a friend for Sunday night dinner and passed out on the bar stool. I fell on the floor.

On one of these trips, I went for a drive in Buckhead with my sister-in-law. It was pouring rain, but we drove on and passed the governor's mansion, and, across the street, my rich friend's richer mother's house. My brother's wife asked me to pull over; she wanted to talk. She told me that, while it was true that she had always hated me, she had seen in recent weeks that I had a good side and she hoped we could go on to be friends. I was very touched, although it lasted about six months, after which she hated me as much if not more than ever, going around to parties in my own hometown saying horrible things about me, saying that somehow I had robbed my brother of his inheritance — they both seemed to be given to these archaic phrases, as though they were characters out of Faulkner — and trying to turn my own relatives and friends against me. My friends and relatives, of course, immediately reported all these remarks to me.

She really seemed to have found her element. She was pregnant, her husband was a brilliant comatose journalist, and she was, as she had always been, the absolute center of attention. But never had the focus of solicitude been turned so absolutely and single-mindedly on her. The story of her situation could soften the most jaundiced heart. There was nothing people wouldn't do for her, run errands, feed her, take her for drives when they knew she hated their guts, and so on.

After awhile, I didn't go any more. I meant to, but I didn't. I said I couldn't get away from work, but that wasn't the real reason. I said I couldn't afford the flight, but I was charging it all anyway, so that wasn't it. It took me years to pay it off. I was making $75,000 a year, not exactly F-class income. But Delta loved me. Every Thursday night the stewardess would ask me if I wanted the usual, fixing me a stiff gin and tonic in a real glass glass before the plane even took off.

The truth was, I couldn't stand her and I didn't trust her, and I didn't want my brother to have married her, but he had, while she was wearing a bias-cut satin dress my mother and grandmother had made, and which she had had them make all over again, stamping her foot because she didn't like the way it fit, causing her own aunt to warn my mother about her the night before the wedding, saying she had always been selfish. It was sweet Minnie Lee Lee who wasn't Chinese whispering these confidences to my mother at the rehearsal dinner, while Judy Judy, in a black cocktail dress and a lot of opera-length pearls, flirted and let all the men look down her cleavage. And while I didn't want my brother to be lying in a hospital room with cheesy breath and thin white arms and the stink of death about him, you can only be so assiduous about even the most terrible grief for so long.

He was paralyzed and speechless but he wasn't dying, so he

was moved away from Elvis and into his own room. Elvis must have been in excruciating pain all the time. By now he was sedated against the pain. Morphined to the gills. My brother wasn't in any pain at all.

My sister-in-law finally had the baby, in the same hospital, and she and the little redheaded girl were taken in a wheelchair down to my brother's room so he could see his daughter. He didn't even open his eyes.

The next morning, the nurse went in to draw the blinds and feed him his breakfast. My brother suddenly sat up in bed and said, "Can you tell me something? I know I've been kind of out of it for awhile, and I missed Wimbledon, so there's something I want to know. Who won the ladies' finals?"

The shocked nurse answered him, Chrissie Evert or whoever, Martina, somebody, and then she asked him, "How did you do that?"

"Do what?"

"Sit up in bed. Talk."

"I don't know. It seemed like it was time."

"You know you have a baby? A little girl?"

"I know," said my brother. "I saw her yesterday."

And after that he never went backward. He only got better. He never got worse. But he was never the same again. Ever. Never the same.

Burn

When my brother and sister and I were children, men and women had two things we don't have now: cocktails and hairdos. They had Gimlets and Manhattans and Gibsons and Singapore Slings and Vodka Stingers and Blue Mondays and Grasshoppers and Old Fashioneds and Highballs and Sidecars. They had Mint Juleps for Derby Day. They also had muddlers and swizzle sticks. Men were known and even famous for their ability to make one or the other of these cocktails. Women never made them, except maybe during the war, they did, when they were alone. But not as well.

It was a whole male ritual of equipment and liquor and deft hand gestures and quips. My father and his friends would say things like "Let me freshen that up for you." They would say things like "grease cutter" and "Just have a nightcap and then you can go."

People had bars that stood out in the open, on fancy pieces of furniture. They had silver ice buckets. They had silver julep cups. They had Highball glasses with their monograms on them. They got these things for wedding presents.

Nowadays, except for the trendy run at a Cosmopolitan or a

Mojito or something, people drink wine. Or hard liquor on Wall Street. When I was little nobody drank wine; they hardly even drank it at dinner, except for very fancy dinner parties. And it was bad wine. At least it was bad wine in the country. It came in jugs. They had cocktails instead. Nobody even says *cocktails* nowadays.

After dinner parties, at which the women wore taffeta or silk dinner dresses, at which they wore earrings and necklaces and clever dinner rings, my mother used to have a tray of cordials with tiny glasses she would bring out, crème de menthe and Triple Sec and Drambuie and cognac and Cherry Heering. Sometimes she would make pousse-café, an amazingly complicated thing she learned about in *Gourmet* that involved layering cordials according to their various densities, so you ended up with a vertical rainbow of six or seven liqueurs. It was like being the Marie Curie of after-dinner drinks. I still have all the fancy little cordial glasses.

The women had hairdos, then. Not haircuts — hairdos. They would wear their hair up or down, in braids, in French twists, in bouffant concoctions, according to the various occasions. They put their hair in rollers in the afternoons, before a party, but they never went to the grocery store with their hair in rollers, just bobby pins sometimes, and their hair sparkled from the hair spray used to hold it all in place.

It was very different then. People in the country lived the kind of life they imagined being lived in the pages of the *New Yorker* magazine. And they were good at it, and it gave them pleasure to be good at it.

People had real parties. My mother and father would grab at any excuse for a cocktail party or a dinner party. Anywhere people were gay and bright and didn't have a care in the world.

They once gave a going-away party for a couple who were going to Europe for two months in the summer. Napoleon came to be the bartender, making cocktails, macerating mint and sugar in the bottom of silver julep cups, serving up Old Fashioneds and Highballs, and the women wore raw silk summer dresses or sleeveless linen dresses with shoes that matched, and some even wore gloves and even hats, and everybody looked like they had a lot of money, even if they didn't have a dime and had just charged it all at J. Ed Deaver or Grossman's, the two local clothing stores for grownups.

There were rules, then. My mother, for instance, never drank or served rum. That was a rule. Nobody had even heard of tequila, then.

My mother was lovely in her bones, as the poem says. She could sew, and so she could make beautiful dresses out of Liberty lawn or linen or, once, gray wool with a jeweled collar. She wore them well. She didn't have any money, but she was always turned out beautifully. She had a friend whose sister or somebody lived in Ohio and bought her clothes at the Dayton Oval Room, and, every now and then, a box would arrive with this woman's castoffs, which wouldn't fit my mother's friend, so my mother had some clothes with fancy designer labels like Pauline Trigere.

At the going-away party, all the guests looked like they didn't have a care in the world. Men stood on the back terrace and told jokes in the waning sunlight and talked about the war and the Virginia Military Institute. Women talked about books or poetry or the garden club. They talked, but they didn't talk dirty. My mother once told me that she'd never heard a woman say *fuck* until after the men came back from World War II, and even then they never said it in public.

A lot of them had grown up together. They had had adventures. My mother and her friend Sunshine and my godmother Emily and my other godmother, Fran Pancake, true, would sometimes talk about the week they had spent at Virginia Beach when they were young, sunning themselves and drinking what they called Scotch-type whiskey. They never tired of talking about that trip, and it was always funny. I saw photographs. They were on the beach, wearing very dark glasses, like blind people in bathing suits.

We heard the stories because we would work the parties. My brother and sister and I would dress up and we would pass things, little cheese straws and cucumber sandwiches with the edges cut off. My mother made this dip for which she was famous. It was made of crabmeat and sherry and Cheez Whiz, and people thought it was delicious, so a lot of them would hover around the dining room table where the chafing dish was. Imagine having a chafing dish.

Their names are the stuff of legend to me. They were the grownups, and I more than anything wanted to be a grownup. Jack Leary, the first man I ever saw naked, who would always get drunk. His wife, Sunshine. Mack and Mary Monroe. Jack and Kyle. The Tutwilers, Ann and Tut. Tommy and George. Movie stars. Might as well have been movie stars.

Sunshine was a sardonic woman. She was stuck in a bad marriage to Jack, a terrible drunk, so she took a very ironic view of life, bitter, of course. I used to spend the night at their house a lot— her children were my best friends—and I saw it all. Once they set the chimney on fire. The fire department came and sprayed water down the chimney. It was over way too soon. Jack was the only man who ever spanked me, except for my father. He spanked his son and me for riding our bicycles in the street in front of the Kappa Sig house. My father didn't really have the heart for it. Jack did. Their house is sold now. So's the Kappa Sig house, actually.

Once my mother passed Sunshine at a stoplight, it was just before Christmas, and my mother leaned out and called, "What do you want for Christmas?" And Sunshine answered, without a trace of a smile, "Out." My mother drove on.

I came home from a birthday party once, having drunk too much punch, and then I threw up on the floor and Sunshine was out for drinks and all she said was, "Listen to me. If it's purple, don't drink it."

See. Cocktails. They knew their stuff.

At parties, at cocktail parties, nothing bad happened. Except sometimes this one woman got embarrassingly drunk and once even had to spend the night, because she fell down on the coffee table and knocked it all to hell and her husband wouldn't even take her home. But usually, nobody said a mean thing and went home before they got too drunk to drive.

Everybody smiled, and kissed each other, and the men got drunk but not too drunk and spilled whiskey on their neckties and wrapped their beefy arms around one another's shoulders and people took black-and-white photographs of all the people in their dense perfection. It was proof that matter can, in fact, be created out of nothing.

The going-away party at which Napoleon came to mix the cocktails was a huge success. It was for some rich people my parents knew, a man who taught with my father and his wife. They were going to Europe on a boat, on the *Queen Elizabeth,* while everybody else would be sweltering in the heat and driving twelve miles for a swim at Goshen Pass, but there was not a trace of envy. People were glad for them; they had a lot of money and close family connections in Richmond. The wife wasn't the shiniest nickel in the bag, but she had a sable coat. At Christmas, she spread it out on the coat bed for all the other women to see when they put down their wool coats.

In those days, it was good manners for the guests of honor to leave first. That was the signal that the party was going to be over soon. As they were leaving, my brother and I were supposed to help them with their coats and whatever things they had brought. The *Queen Elizabeth* couple had a twenty-year-old daughter, and she had worn a small mink stole to the party, a summer fur, I guess they were called, probably borrowed from her mother or her grandmother. Her grandmother had real money. The small mink stole was so soft. It felt so expensive.

My mother had a mink coat. It was short and light brown. She won it in a contest in which she was asked to describe the goodness of a certain brand of split pea soup. Every day, when my father came home from graduate school, she would serve him split pea soup. She wouldn't eat it herself, because she loathed it, but he would describe it to her, and then she would sit all afternoon—she was pregnant with my brother at the time—and she would compose twenty-five words or less in praise of this whatever split pea soup. She won. They were so poor, they had to ask his mother for money to pay the taxes on the coat. My mother loved that coat.

So I was helping the daughter on with the stole, putting it around her shoulders, and she turned and said, "Why, thank you, honey. You'll make somebody a nice little wife someday." Why would anybody say that to an eight-year-old boy?

She lives in Vermont now. She's old, I guess, and a widow, but her words are still a complete curiosity in my memory. Maybe she just wasn't very adept, like her mother.

My mother and father were not only good at giving parties, generous and clever, they were good at going to parties. People adored them for their wit and charm, for their lean good looks, for the way my mother dressed, and my father, too. My mother never wore anything that didn't show off her slender waist. She had a lot of belts.

She smoked, and she did it eloquently, and she was not only funny, she was witty, intelligently witty. We had a minister in our church named Barrett, and once, when my mother knelt at the altar rail as he approached with the chalice, she looked up at him with an innocent, pious expression and said so anybody nearby could hear, she said, "Pass the claret, Barrett." That kind of thing. She wrote witty occasional poems for people's birthdays, and people treasured her company.

This was before it all went bad. This was before she started dressing in wash-and-wear pants and blouses from Leggett's, before she stopped caring, before she stopped sewing, before her conversation turned vague and unfocused.

They were a handsome couple, my parents, and they lived in a charming house that belonged to my mother's mother. My mother always sat in the same chair, a blue slipper chair by the fireplace, and she claimed she was always cold, even in the hot, muggy summers, possibly because she so rarely ate anything.

She had cigarettes and coffee for breakfast, she had cottage cheese and canned pears and cigarettes for lunch, she never ate bread or dessert. She never ate between meals. She was thin but not painfully so and that's why she looked so good in clothes. She said she'd been fat as a child and she never wanted to be fat again.

Once, when she was a child, she got run over by a car. It was one of those light, early cars — she was born in 1919 — and she wasn't hurt at all, but my panicked grandfather told her she could have anything she wanted. He felt responsible. His eye had strayed for a minute.

She said she wanted to have her hair cut like a boy's.

Almost every day, people came for drinks, or my parents went somewhere else for drinks. When you went somewhere else for drinks, not cocktail parties, just everyday drinks, you always took your own liquor.

When people went out for drinks, they'd take their children with them, and we'd play together, unless they were girls, in which case they'd play with my sister. One little girl had a doll baby named Horrible. Horrible had lost all of her hair — some of it burned off with matches — and many of her body parts and one of her eyes and was in every way hideous, but this little girl loved Horrible, or Harble, as she would say, and wouldn't give her up. At our house we'd play games because we didn't have a TV. That's why we liked it when we went out for drinks with my parents. Other kids had TVs. We could watch whatever we wanted.

My father had an ice tapper, a kind of bendable rod with a heavy metal disk at the end, and this was his way of breaking up ice cubes. You could set your watch by it. Five o'clock, the tapping of the ice cracker signaled the beginning of the cocktail hour.

Somebody once said to me that all families were either about the parents or about the children, and ours was about the parents. More exactly, it was about the cocktail and dinner hour, my mother always smartly dressed, my father smoking, but only after five o'clock. He could smoke a pack of cigarettes between five o'clock and bedtime, but he only smoked the first inch of a cigarette, which was great when we were older and started learning to smoke, the ashtrays filled with these cigarettes that were almost whole. My mother never dumped the ashtrays at night; she was afraid of fires.

In Virginia, we generally started smoking secretly about age fifteen; we started smoking in front of our parents at sixteen, and the idea was, you just kept on smoking until you died. Cigarettes cost a quarter a pack.

My parents believed you learned to drink at home. When I was seventeen and started sitting with the grownups for the cocktail hour, my parents didn't like it that I didn't drink, so they'd buy these sissy aperitifs like Lillet, like Cherry Heering, like Dubonnet, hoping I'd like them. When I was seventeen, my mother and I decided to cut down on smoking, so we started smoking pipes, and I would sit with the grownups, smoking a pipe and gagging my way through a glass of Lillet on the crushed rocks.

My mother wore gloves. Her fingernails were scarlet, her

mouth was scarlet. She wore a perfume, Wind Song, by Prince Matchabelli. She loved Joy, and sometimes my father would give her a small bottle for Christmas. Later, when I moved to New York, I started buying her Norell, and she liked that a lot. She didn't wear Wind Song in its little crown-shaped bottle anymore. She had no idea what Norell cost. She thought it was probably about the same.

When she died, there was a bottle of Norell on her dressing table. She hadn't worn it in so long it had turned amber and viscous and you could barely get the top off.

She wore powder, and her dressing table was always covered with a thin, dusty layer of pale pink. She was publicly elegant, but privately slovenly, even then.

She bathed in the late afternoon, changing for cocktails, and once, in the bathtub, she pulled a rusted carpet tack out of her rib cage. She showed it to us; she showed it to the people who came for drinks. She lifted up her blouse to show the little hole it came out of. Once, during the cocktail hour, she sat down in a chair right on a pair of scissors, which plunged through her girdle and deep into her behind.

My mother was the last woman in the world to need a girdle, she was so thin and gamine, but she always wore one.

She ran from the room, blood streaming, and went upstairs to my grandmother's room, the scissors still imbedded in her bleeding flesh. My grandmother told her to turn around, and she put one foot up on my mother's ass—it feels odd saying my mother's ass, but I don't know what else to call it. She pulled the scissors out as though she were pulling off a riding boot. My grandmother put on some iodine and a bandage, she had been a nurse, and my mother changed her dress and went back downstairs to cocktails. She had to sit sideways, but it made for a really funny story, anyway, right away. Just one of those funny things that happened at cocktails when the whoevers were out last week.

Later, when I started working, she started to ask me to buy clothes for her in New York. I bought them at Bonwit Teller or Bergdorf Goodman. My mother would send me a hundred dollars and ask me to get her a dress for a wedding or a dance or some big party. Even in those days, you couldn't buy a dress for a hundred dollars, so I'd buy whatever I thought would look nice on her, whatever it cost. For my sister's wedding, I bought her a long green Oscar de la Renta dress, a perfect garden party kind of dress, and I told her it cost a hundred dollars. It cost eight hundred dollars. I told her I'd bought it at a discount outlet. When she took up the hem, there was a tape I hadn't noticed that said BERGDORF GOODMAN over and over around the whole full long skirt. She didn't bat an eyelash.

I liked to see my mother in beautiful clothes. I wanted to believe we were richer than we were, and my parents were so unhappy that I would do almost anything to please them, although, as many people have told me, they never showed the slightest pride or gratitude for anything I'd done.

Once, when I was in college, a roommate said to me on the ride back to school after a weekend at home, "I have a question. You have a 4.0 average, you've just won a big fellowship, you're giving a speech at graduation, you have the most beautiful girlfriend of anybody. Where's the pride? Where's the *nachus*? If I'd done what you did, my mother would take out a full-page ad in the *New York Times*."

We just did what we did because that's what we were expected to do, and we wanted to please them, to do anything to break this chain of bitterness and depression that hung over the house when all the guests were gone. My mother took tranquilizers, like all housewives did then, and she longed to have a job. She had a job before we were born, working in the lab at the hospital, but my father didn't like it, so she stopped, and went on just wearing beautiful dresses and scarlet lipstick and making exquisite dinners when company came.

She made a dessert called tortoni, which was a sort of coffee *semifreddo*. I hated it, but it wasn't for children anyway, like avocados. Avocados were too expensive, alligator pears, so we were told children wouldn't like them.

She made a cake that was called Paris-Brest because it was invented on a train in France. She made the best biscuits in town, better even than my grandmother's, although she never ate a single one. At the end of the month, when the money was all gone, she made Welsh rarebit. She kept her household money in a book called *The Pleasures of Poverty*, and when that was almost gone, she made creamed chipped beef on toast. She had three hundred dollars a month to feed a family of five. But at the beginning of the month, she rubbed flour on roasts of beef so the skin would be crispy.

Everybody was poor. They were all college professors and they were always borrowing fifty dollars or a fifth of bourbon to get them to the end of the month. My parents may have run out of money, but they never ran out of bourbon, and the ice tapper would still go off at five o'clock, even on the last day of the month, even if we were eating Welsh rarebit for dinner, even if they had to borrow fifty dollars from my grandmother.

It was all about perfection. My mother and father presented a perfect picture to the world, a happy, witty, and charming young couple who were madly in love, and did nothing but have fun.

My mother would get dressed to go out to an evening party, and she would come out into the central hall upstairs to brightly call goodnight to us. Our bedrooms opened into the hall, or at least mine did and my sister's did, and my brother would come and sit on my bed to watch her say goodnight. Sometimes, most of the time, she would come in and we'd say our prayers, and sometimes she'd sing "Lavender Blue," or "Oralee," which had the same tune as "Love Me Tender," and then she'd stand for a second in the upstairs hall, as my father stood impatiently at the bottom of the stairs.

As she stood there, my sister would call out from her bed, "Twirl, Mama, twirl," and my mother would twirl, like a runway model, and we'd watch her skirts billow and her scarlet lips and her scarlet fingernails and the light brown hair my father once described as beige. It was her gift to us, her final goodnight kiss, and we loved her for it.

One summer night, when it was still twilight outside, my father called from the bottom of the stairs and she came out of her room in a sleeveless dress made of something blue, probably fake silk, that had a layer of chiffon over it. It had green and blue stripes on it, and the stripes were diagonal, going one way on the top and the other way on the bottom.

"Twirl, Mama, twirl," my sister called out, and she did, twice around, and the stripes blurred, like a funfair whirligig that you can't focus on once it starts moving. Then she blew us a kiss, and told us to say our prayers, and then her high heels clattered down the steps.

"Jesus Christ," my father said. "It's after eight o'clock already," and then they were gone.

This is the prayer we used to say, every night: "O Lord support us, all the day long, till the shadows lengthen and the evening comes and the busy world is hushed and our work is done and the fever of life is over; then in thy mercy grant us a safe lodging, a holy rest, and peace at the last. Amen." We loved all those *ands* in a row. I still say it, every night, even when I feel I've lost my faith forever and God has already abandoned me a long time ago.

Ten minutes later, we heard her rush up the stairs, and she went into her closet in the hall and then into her bedroom and came out ten minutes later in another dress. I don't remember the second dress and my sister didn't call out and she didn't twirl for us that time, just rushed off as though we weren't there.

We were shocked. My sister and brother and I got out of our beds and crept into my mother and father's room and there, lying on the bed, was the dress with the blue and green stripes. We looked at it. We looked at it closely because we didn't understand what could possibly have happened. Then we saw it.

On the skirt, on the blue and green skirt with the diagonal stripes going the other way, there was a burn hole the size of a dime. You could see the turquoise underskirt through it. Obviously, she had been smoking in the car and dropped a cigarette ash on the dress and the ash had burned a small hole in the chiffon part. It wasn't perfect anymore. She couldn't wear it.

We went to sleep and we never saw the dress again.

It was such a tiny, tiny thing. My mother smoked. She smoked in the car, her scarlet lipstick staining the filter. It was a gorgeous summer evening and they were on their way to a lovely party and they looked beautiful and my mother smoked in the car and burned a hole in the skirt of a blue and green dress. A tiny thing.

But it meant something had happened. Maybe they had a fight. They often did, terrible vitriolic fights. My brother would go to the top of the stairs and call out, "Please don't fight, Mama and Daddy. Please don't fight," and my mother would come to the bottom of the stairs and look at her frightened son and say sweetly, "We're not fighting. We're just having a discussion, darling. Now go back to bed," and he would and they would go back to yelling at each other. Too many drinks, drinks after dinner and my mother's bitterness at her own failures — she had wanted to be a poet — and my father's failures — he had never finished his thesis. All this would come out and they would yell at each other.

But something had happened in the car. Something had happened to her beautiful dress, there had been some tiny, visible flaw created in the perfection of the whole, which couldn't be allowed, some visible unhappiness, and we never understood it and we never asked because we never asked anything and we never forgot it.

We loved our parents, our mother whom everybody adored

and our handsome father whose hair turned snow white by the time he was forty. We loved them and we were afraid of them. We were afraid because we knew they were unhappy.

I used to think that there was something I could do to make it all right. I knew, somehow, that it was my fault, and I knew I could find the key to their unhappiness and open the door into a glorious world. I knew then we could all be happy and forgiven for the shame of being unhappy.

I used to concoct these ridiculous schemes. Every year around September, I began to dream that I could give them something for Christmas that would make a difference. I would build my father a boat. I would make my mother a diamond necklace. I would make detailed drawings in secret. With my twenty-five dollar Christmas allowance, I would find some gem dealer who would be willing to sell me lesser diamonds and I would learn jewelry making and my mother would be amazed on Christmas morning and my father would have a sleek sailboat and everything would be OK forever.

It never worked, and I always ended up getting my mother some costume jewelry brooch at Leggett's that she never wore, and my father got handkerchiefs or a tie or a belt. No diamonds. No boat. And I was always heartbroken at my failure. I knew a brooch or a belt wouldn't make any difference.

When I was fourteen, and had made some money in the summer mowing lawns and pulling weeds, I had my own checking account, and I sent away to Georg Jensen in New York for six crystal water goblets. My parents loved them, but it didn't matter. I still have four of them. When I was fifteen, I sent a check for twenty-five dollars to Andrew Wyeth and told him I knew it wasn't much, but maybe he could send me a sketch he didn't have any use for because my parents loved his work so much.

I waited in a panic for his reply, and it finally came, a nice note with a drawing of his house in Chadds Ford on it. He returned my check. My father showed the letter to everybody and then he had it laminated, destroying its value, and he had it framed in a cheap frame and hung it where everybody could see it and think what a funny and charming little fool I was.

When I was thirty, after my grandmother had died and the house my mother grew up in, the house we all grew up in, went into her estate, I bought it and gave it to my parents as a gift for their lifetime. My mother never even said thank you.

Nothing worked. They went on fighting in private and being charming in public, although some people began to see through the facade. One friend of theirs wrote in his photograph album, beneath a picture of the house I was later to buy, "When I first knew these people, I thought they were brilliant and beautiful and their house a magical place. Then I began to see them as ordinary and, finally, pathetic." My brother saw it. He said later it was the exact thing that caused him to fall apart into his quiet madness some years later. I don't know why anybody would write a thing like that in a photograph album.

She had burned a hole in her dress and we had, for the first time, seen through the veil of perfection. That was all.

It's funny the things we remember when there's so much we forget. We remember them in no particular order, and most of them we can't put a value on.

My mother was good to us. Even when we had no money,

and she served Welsh rarebit, she served it out of a silver chafing dish. Sometimes, when we had no money, she would make waffles on a waffle iron at the dinner table set with repoussé silver. And those memories are good ones.

When I was twenty-four, I wrote a novel. It was called "Documents of the Sleeper." It is dense and abstract and turgid beyond belief and it was about my family and my brother getting thrown out of Williams at the end of his junior year. That's at least what I thought it was about, at the time. I had written what I thought was a happy ending, although there was, by then, no hope for a happy ending. I wrote about the dress and about my sister saying "Twirl, Mama, twirl." I wrote about scenes of our life, nothing terrible, but private moments that were less than perfect.

There was a family law that we didn't talk about the family outside in the world, didn't reveal the slightest crack in the facade, and I had broken the law.

I couldn't afford to have it typed in New York, so I had a red-haired girl I'd grown up with type it at home. I paid her a hundred dollars. She was Sunshine's daughter, as a matter of fact. My mother kept bugging her, so she showed the first hundred pages to my parents, and that was when all hell broke loose.

The phone calls stopped. The letters stopped, my mother's frequent and charming letters. My father had already disinherited me — not that he had any money to leave, but, two years before, I had been living in Greece and I wanted to borrow three hundred dollars to get home. I wrote to my father, who responded that I was a disgusting lazy pig and "never in my lifetime or after will you ever receive a penny of my money." See?

They talked like people out of a Victorian novel. I had paid for
my own college education, with scholarships and borrowed
money, I had won a fellowship to study in Europe, won it twice
in fact, and still I was the one who was a disgusting pig.

My father often complained about how hard he worked. He
had three weeks off at Christmas, three weeks in the spring, and,
generally, when he didn't teach summer school because we
needed the money, he had the whole summer off. He was home
every day by lunchtime. He took a nap every afternoon. He never
bought a house of his own. He never picked up a sock. Still, I was
the one who was lazy. I was the one who was disgusting.

After he disinherited me, we went on as though nothing had
happened. I borrowed the money from my grandmother and
went home for Christmas. Christmas was just like it always was,
and nobody said anything about anything. I went to New York
for a New Year's Eve party, on the bus, and decided to stay and
find a job. When I first started working, I couldn't believe you
were expected to work fifty weeks a year. It seemed barbaric.

Finally, after six weeks, there was a phone call, and I was sum-
moned home. I had to buy my own plane ticket. I was making
$25,000 a year then. I had just moved into the disgusting walkup
I went on to live in for almost sixteen years.

I was afraid. I was afraid of my parents. I was more afraid of
my mother, whose rages and torments were unpredictable, than
I was of my father, whose main behavior was righteous indigna-
tion. Dickensian bluster and spoiled meanness were what he did
best, when he wasn't busy being charming. Well, he had lost a
lot, I guess, the brilliant future lost through laziness and ennui,
the brilliant wife turned brilliantly cold and bitter, the whole

sense of entitlement a lie that he was never too drunk to forget. He was a fool and a failure, and, like most people in middle age, the deceptions were harder and harder to pull off. All he had left was a thin veneer of charm, and there were fewer and fewer new people to tell the old anecdotes to.

I once knew a woman who shot her husband and then killed herself because she was scheduled to give a cocktail party two days later and realized, as they lay in bed, her husband asleep by her side, that their lives were so hopelessly lost to debt and drugs and liquor and terrible, terrible sadness, that she could not produce the illusion, like a magician who had run out of rabbits.

My father didn't even have the strength to realize how out of control it all was; he just went on, anecdote to anecdote, and he and my mother fought over after-dinner drinks and the mornings were foul and the naps were clammy and his sweat smelled musty and foul but he went on, because that's what gentlemen did, and he wasn't a drunk like his father, which was a lie, even if his posture was perfect, his hair snow white, his lips pursing as though he were kissing somebody as he leaned into his next sip of bourbon.

The battle took place after dinner, when the round of drinks had been made. Grease cutters. My mother had changed into a long quilted blue bathrobe, and she curled up in a chair, her legs under her, while my father smoked an inch of a hundred cigarettes and it went on for hours and it was excruciating. They loathed me with such a palpability it is difficult to recall.

When I was a teenager, we went to parties every night in the summer. Most nights, we had parties at our house. We'd drag the old cabinet record player out into the back yard, and hook it up with a long extension cord and we'd lie around with our friends, listening to Dylan, the older ones drinking Pabst Blue Ribbon, which we just thought the coolest thing since pockets in shirts. People would bring guitars, and we'd sing old ballads out of Alan Lomax, and in the morning, my mother would always ask whether anybody had gone bundling, meaning making out in the box bushes. She was glad to have the house filled with young people. They all adored her, and she'd sit up in her bathrobe and they'd go in, one by one, and talk to her.

We once had a party one New Year's Eve, my brother and I, in my grandmother's part of the house. My parents had some friends over for drinks, all the women in long skirts and fancy jewelry, like something out of a movie about charming sophisticates, all gay chatter by the fire in another part of the house, the part our family lived in. At one point, I opened the door to the room where the grownups were and my mother said, "What are you all doing?"

"We're pretending we're drunk," I said.

"We're pretending we're not," she said, and I closed the door.

She didn't like it as much when we went out. In the morning she'd always ask what we talked about. This and that, we'd say, stuff. "Did you talk about us?" she'd ask. "Did you talk about me?" We would stare at one another in disbelief.

She'd listened to all those young people telling how their parents didn't understand them, or wouldn't let them do the one thing they had their hearts set on, and she was always sympathetic, the mother everybody wanted to have. She let my sister fly to Mexico on her own when she was seventeen. She gave all our friends the illusion that she uniquely understood their teenaged torture, the illusion that she would have let any of them do anything: take drugs, move to France, get married. But she was terrified that her children talked about her behind her back. "Did you talk about us?"

I had talked about them, in the novel, and the sin was unforgivable. The incidents were trivial, there was nothing particularly revealing in the small anecdotes in the book, but things that were private had been made public.

I had written about how trapped women must feel, left alone all day in houses filled with possessions they had to care for but could never really own. I had talked about a present my brother once found for her, the most marvelous present ever, and he'd found it on Christmas Eve—a nineteenth-century Tiffany ladies' traveling case, covered in leather and filled with crystal bottles with vermeil cloisonné tops and hairbrushes and a sewing kit and buttonhooks for shoes and dresses, a toothbrush still in its crystal flask with its lavender enameled top, the whole thing incredibly stamped with my mother's initials. My brother had found it in Ray Miller's junk shop on Christmas Eve and bought it for twenty-five dollars and I, with all my mail order passions and my dreams of diamonds and yachts, was more jealous than I had ever been of anything. It was perfection, and it made my mother impossibly happy, and it was only by luck, which my brother had and I did not.

And I had written about the cigarette burn in the green and blue dress. I hadn't commented, I had only reported. I didn't understand its power then and I don't now, but I had told the story and my mother remembered it. She objected, screaming at me, to my telling family stories, to my telling things about the family that the world didn't know. There was little chance that the book would be published—even my mother pointed out that it was obtuse and overwritten—but that wasn't the point.

I had talked about her.

The tirade went on so long my father had to refill their drinks several times, the ice tapper tapping out its familiar sound. He would scream at me from the bar in the pantry. He would say things like, "How dare you!" The kind of things offended debutantes might say in movies of the thirties, before they slapped Adolph Menjou or somebody in the face. The more my mother and father drank, the more insane with anger they got.

By this time, they weren't young anymore. Everybody went to Europe. Nobody gave going-away parties. Nobody had weddings with twelve bridesmaids, each one wearing a different colored pastel linen dress with a matching cartwheel hat. Even we had a television by then.

The wear and tear on them showed in their faces and in the way they dressed and the way their cleaning ladies had left them, and their napkins weren't pressed. It showed in the fact that women didn't wear gloves or carry clean white embroidered handkerchiefs in their purses, and men didn't wear ties in the evenings when they went out for drinks. It showed in jaundice and cirrhosis of the liver. The children all had long hair and smoked dope and took acid, although we, my brother and sister and I, still wrote our own mother thank-you notes if we came home for the weekend.

One couple had run through all her money because he was a book salesman who couldn't sell any books, and they were se-

cretly selling her priceless possessions through an auction house
in New York. She had real pearls, and emeralds. She had two
dozen of the czar's napkins, two feet square, embroidered with
the Romanov seal. Sunshine's husband had gone to the rehab
place several times without success, and she had left him and
was having an affair with a married local doctor. Men had
beaten their wives, and their wives had left them. Wives revealed
they had slept around during the war and their heartbroken hus-
bands had gone away.

The life that happened when the doors closed was becoming
more and more distant from the lives led in public, although the
afternoon drinks went on, the bars were still stocked and ready,
but my mother didn't serve liqueurs or make pousse-café anymore. There was less to celebrate. For some, there was nothing
to celebrate, only the monotony of making do, of going on with
it, of boring themselves to death.

And maybe the green and blue dress stood for something that
had existed long before any of that. Maybe the dress stood for a
kind of perfection that was no longer attainable, even as an illusion. Youth fades. We are never where we meant to be, and it
always seems hollow and stupid and a waste of time. We become, finally, the biggest burden we have to bear, the burden of
our own known selves.

And maybe twirling for her children was something my
mother realized was from another time, a place she couldn't get
back to, like the woman who realized she could no longer have
seventy-five people over for drinks. Her house was simply too
dirty, and she was simply too tired to clean it. And they couldn't
pay for it.

It was eleven o'clock. This harangue had been going on for three hours, and every one of my failures had been recounted. My mother finally asked, with steely sobriety, "Why did you write this book?"

I didn't know. I mumbled something fatuous, something about how close we were as a family, and how we'd gone through a lot with my brother, and I wanted to do something that would heal the pain. I wanted to make you a diamond necklace, I wanted to say. I wanted to build you a boat. I pointed out that the book had a happy ending they hadn't seen, a healing conclusion in which we were all perfect and perfectly happy. I don't know if that was true, but I said it. My mother said she wouldn't read another word of this trash.

"I was always happy," my mother said. "I'll never be happy again."

I said that I had written the book because children needed to do something finally, to stand on their own two feet, to cut the ties that bound them so suffocatingly to the parents they loved.

"I'll tell you why you wrote it," my mother said. "You wrote it because you're wicked. You were born wicked. You're wicked now. You'll die wicked." And then she got unsteadily to her feet and went to bed. I can still smell the way she smelled as she passed, the face powder that never got taken off, only added to, the dirty bathrobe, the underclothes, the hard iron smell of a woman who isn't clean, who had pulled a carpet tack out of her rib cage.

My father retreated into silence, smoking cigarette after cigarette. She was the whole reason for his anger, and she had gone to bed. I had nothing to say to him. I meant nothing to him.

I left the house and got in the car and drove twelve miles out

to the river, where I sat on the rocks in the dark, the smell of
dark soft pine and wet rocks, the place where I had been swimming and been so happy as a child, when we were all happy,
sleeping overnight in Sunshine's or Fran Pancake's cedar cabins
with no running water and no electricity, the children telling
ghost stories by flashlight, while the grownups drank grease cutters by the flickering light of kerosene lamps.

I knew what I had done. I knew my mother was right. It was
both a curse and a factual recounting of all I had been to her, of
all I had been, and the night wrapped around me like a snake-
skin I couldn't shed.

It was just a dress. It was just a cigarette hole in the dress. But
something had happened, something had been irrevocably lost,
and I have never known what it was.

Playing the Zone

When I was in the loony bin, the hospital had two wings. One was for drunks. The other was for crazy people. I was in the ward for crazy people. The door was always locked, and we were constantly watched for suicidal behavior, but I found it comforting. It wasn't so much that I was locked in; it was that everybody else was locked out. That was a relief.

Compared to the only other mental hospital I had seen, this one was kind of nice, considering you were a prisoner and everything. It was built like a college dorm, with neat hallways and an office at the end where you went to get your meds, and clean spare modern rooms with linoleum floors and two twin beds and a shower and bars on the windows. Nice.

We never saw the ward where the drunk people and the drug addicts were. I think they weren't locked in.

I was kind of a star, because I had come all that way from New York, from a place, they believed, where anybody could get magical psychiatric help. Everybody there was depressed; we were a bunch of thin, etiolated neurasthenic possible suicides, and we felt very sorry for ourselves and we felt genuinely sorry for each other. Somehow, other people's craziness had a more palpable reality than our own, and, as fucked up as we were, we were constantly moved at how irrationally pitiful other people's lives could get.

I was also a star because of the viciousness and multiplicity of the cuts on my arms, cuts that should have been stitched, that were bathed in Betadine and swathed in bandages. They had all seen them, though. Right after I checked into the ward, I was sat down in the common room and a nurse started to draw some blood. I'm not sure what they wanted to know. I fainted, just as the whole ward got back from lunch and saw everything. Imagine, after all that cutting, I fainted when they drew blood. I couldn't think of anything but my longing for the razor blade, and still I fainted. I couldn't figure it out.

The first night I was there, I had to hand in any sharp objects I had, the razor blade, the razor, which I could get back for ten minutes every morning to shave, and any medications I had with me. The only thing I had was Afrin nasal spray, to which I was severely addicted.

When I went to bed, I found in my suitcase a short, sharp penknife. It looked to me like something I had never owned, like somebody had planted it there. I debated, then walked down to the nurse's station and handed it in. When I got out of the bin, weeks later, they gave it back to me, and I gave it to my doctor as a present, as a promise, a small silver Tiffany penknife with my initials on it I had never seen before.

The first night I couldn't breathe. The Afrin rebound kicked in, and I spent the night trying to get one clear breath through my nose. The guard would look in on me every now and then, and there I would be, sniffling away.

The next morning, my doctor asked me why I'd been crying

all night. I told him the truth, but I didn't get the Afrin back. He told me I'd get over it and I did.

We had to get up at seven in the morning. We had to get dressed, no shuffling around in bathrobes for us, drooling. We had to make our beds and shower and look as much like normal people as possible.

Most people had roommates. I didn't, because I had said I wouldn't come if I had to have one, and because I was, as I say, sort of a star.

We were let out of the ward three times a day, to go eat, in a large cafeteria where we ate enormous amounts of food. The first week I was there, I gained ten pounds. We lived on starch and carbohydrates, and the food wasn't very good, but there was very little to do, so we ate a lot. And most of the drugs most of us were taking made you gain weight, too. We were led to meals by kindhearted guards, and we were never made to feel ashamed about our various states of despair.

We had group therapy twice a day, once in the morning, and once after dinner, before the meds kicked in. We also had individual therapy once a day. My own doctor was the head of the hospital, and he was brilliant and kind. I wasn't in much of a position to judge, but that's the way he seemed. He asked to see my arms. He told me which cuts should have had stitches. He told me how many stitches.

It wasn't my recent behavior that interested him as much as the causes of my recent behavior, and like a lot of people who are locked up, I was glad to talk, especially about myself.

When you're in the bin, you feel the need to justify yourself.

You feel the need to prove that you really do need to be there, and so you'll say anything so that they'll keep you. That's how glad you are to be locked up.

The other thing we had to do was go to the gym every day. It's amazing what a few endorphins can do for even the most terminally depressed. We were led through exercises by young men and women who looked like something out of a poster for young men and women like that, the kind of people who taught you physical education in grade school. They were strong, they were beautiful, and they were, unlike the ones in grade school, infinitely kind. They didn't look like they were about to have a heart attack at any minute. They seemed like grownups to us, because we seemed like children to ourselves.

When we were in the gym, we got a good look at the drunks and the addicts. They were a scary-looking bunch. They could bench-press four hundred pounds. They could do one-armed push-ups. They were poster children for Guns N' Roses, a bunch of beefy, muscular, tattooed, mean-hearted Kentucky biker rednecks, and they could probably bite the cap off a beer bottle.

We felt a kind of gratitude for the safety of our locked ward. This was not a sentiment shared by the drunks and the drug addicts who wanted in the worst kind of way to be out drinking Jack Black and shooting crystal meth. They were not happy. They looked at us and laughed. They sneered, showing yellowed nicotined teeth.

We were too thin, too wan, and didn't have enough tattoos to command anything other than disdain. And we were, comparatively, so small. Most of us couldn't even do a chin-up.

The worst part was volleyball. After we had finished calis-thenics and the exercise machines, we had to play the drunks and drug addicts in volleyball.

They roared with aggression. They were, every one of them, enraged. They attacked the ball. They attacked the net. They would have attacked us if we in any way had cramped their style. But we were much too intimidated to do anything that might aggravate them. One look at them, and we had already lost the game.

Even with the hearty exhortations of the physical instructors, we couldn't beat them. We couldn't even score a point. We would walk back to the ward after every session, disconsolate with de-feat. "You can do it," the instructors would say. "You'll get 'em to-morrow." We knew these were hollow words meant to get us through the slow hours from defeat to meds. We knew we would never get them.

On the way back from the gym one day, a woman said to me in a gentle drawl, looking at my arms, "Boy, you really did some kind of job on yourself." She smiled. Southerners are always cheered at the sight of somebody else making a spectacle of himself. I felt something like pride.

I took a Rorschach test. I never knew you went through the blobs once, and then again, to see if you said the same thing you said the first time around. If blob number 34 suggested to you your father's hands, it was somehow important that, when you saw blob number 34 again, it still reminded you of your father's hands and not, say, a cypress tree in a drought. It seemed kind of like going to a psychic, but I have to say that the woman's diagnosis was uncannily accurate, like the psychic who tells you you have trouble with money or difficulty with commitment.

She said I suffered from anhedonia, from the Greek, meaning an inability to experience pleasure. Oh, really, I felt like saying. Oh really.

A young guy joined us on the ward, the first new person since I had arrived. He was kept in a room with glass walls next to the nurses' station, and he was so sedated he could barely raise his head from the pillow. We couldn't figure out what was wrong with him, except that he was sad. He hadn't tried to kill himself, at least not in any obvious physical way, but the fact that he was kept in the glass room must have meant that he might, at any moment. He was so depressed, he made the rest of us feel artificial somehow. He was so young and vulnerable and exposed, and his despair was mute and profound, and he made palpable and visible the agony of having a broken heart. It does happen.

We felt afraid for him. We felt for him a tenderness we didn't feel for ourselves. He was probably twenty-four.

We went for supervised walks on the grounds of the hospital. The air was crisp, the weather beautiful the way it almost always is in the middle of tragedy. The way it was after Kennedy was killed. October in Kentucky is heartrendingly beautiful.

It was, I guess, like the first weeks of being at college. We sat together and told our stories, we clumsily embroidered the truth to make ourselves more interesting, like the guys who said they'd gotten into Harvard but had chosen Hopkins instead. The weight of our narrative had a lyrical beauty to it. Most people's stories didn't have a linear quality; their depression was diffuse and nonspecific and awful, just day after day of dread and fear and unquiet.

The doctors listened, and gently explained the causes of depression. They explained how it works on the system, how lassitude and manic energy both become self-fueling fires, winding us up and spinning us out of control, how we lose our appetites, our sense of place, our sense of where we belong in the world, of where it is we are meant to sit down.

I was taking 450 milligrams of Elavil a day, a kind of knee-walking drunk dose, if you don't know. I could barely walk to bed at night. I could barely follow the stories that moved me so much. There was just this veil of human misery over everything, and it made the earthly landscape hard to see.

"How's it going?" "How're you doing today?" In a loony bin, people are always asking you how you're doing, and they pretty much genuinely want to know, as opposed to the normal population outside, who couldn't care less. And the answer usually is, not very well.

When you're in a mental hospital, it's OK to feel bad. That's why you're there. You feel worse, on the average, than the average person will ever know. You're just generally, in the bin, not having a swell day.

I don't think anybody was faking. It wasn't the sort of team you could fake your way onto.

Some people felt like talking. A lot didn't. I didn't particularly want to go into the times and places that had brought me to this time and place. I felt the dozens of wounds on my arms were explanation enough, they stung and they itched and they were my statement that I had been to places lower and more terrifying than any of the rest of them could imagine, with their sad routines and their mundane lives. Measured out in coffee spoons. They suffered, I felt, not from a surfeit but a lack of pain, self-inflicted if need be, but real physical pain to counter the emotional pain. Somehow, even in the bin, you're still competitive. You want to beat out the competition. You want to be the best at what you do, even if what you do is feel miserable and self-destructive all the time. Every minute of every day.

One woman was a psychiatrist. She was there because she had tried to kill herself for the third time. So I wasn't the only one. She was less than thirty-five. She was pretty, and she didn't seem particularly depressed, and she recounted the methods of suicide she had tried, the last being to stick her head in the oven and turn on the gas. Not very effective. She seemed determined that her next try would be her last. I never knew what was the source of her terrible anguish, because as cheerful as she was, she must have felt a great deal of pain.

She was so busy talking about methodology and her blueprint for the future we never got much of a grip on what got her in this state in the first place. She was hopeful for her chances of success on her next attempt, like somebody who's training to swim the Channel.

On top of it all, she really was a psychiatrist. She was a woman who had trained for years to treat crazy people. She had actually, until she began trying to kill herself, treated crazy people, although she said a lot of them were just bored. And she was crazy herself. Suddenly our doctors looked suspect, as though they themselves harbored secret insanities that could come out in various perversities, in the forty Seconal, in the amphetamine addiction, in the sudden break with reality.

The boy from the glass room got out and joined in group therapy. He never said anything. He was on Haldol and Thorazine and God knows what else, we figured, which gave him in our eyes an instant kind of glamour. These were not drugs for babies. As drugged as we were, we were practically perky compared to him.

He had such a sad, forlorn air about him. Handsome, dark, young, pale with grief—the kind of face you remember for a long time. A face that should have been having sex with a girl in the backseat of a car, out by the river, their shirts unbuttoned, their lips swollen with kissing. But his face at the moment was a kind of putty. He was pretty knocked out. He was too medicated to speak. But he listened; he watched us with his glittering eyes, and he slept in a normal room in a normal bed where you could turn the lights out. Now he, too, had to get up every day at seven and follow the regime, drugged and sad as he was.

He joined us in the gym. He was strong and had obviously seen the inside of a gym before. He wasn't intimidated by the rednecks, but he was too blanked out to take much notice of them. Even our thundering defeats in volleyball left him no more fazed than he was already.

Then one night the psychiatrist who had tried to kill herself three times had a brilliant idea. She began, in group therapy, to talk to us about volleyball and addiction.

"The thing about drunks and addicts is they have no sense of limits, they have no sense of boundaries," she explained. "That's why they get to be alcoholics and drug addicts. They don't know when or where to stop." Not that sticking your head in the oven or slitting your own skin open with a razor shows much sense of decorum or control, it now seems to me, but at the time she had our attention.

"Volleyball is a very simple game. There are six people on a side. The court is divided into twelve sections, six on each side of the net. If you notice, if you hit the ball, say, far down to the left side of the court, the average addict will follow the ball. He'll leave his square and follow the ball. They all will. We can beat them."

We didn't believe her, but she was so intent about it we listened anyway.

"If we just play in our squares, if we stick to playing the space assigned to us, we can beat them really, really easily. It's simple. The first person on our team serves the ball all the way down to the right, they all run down there. If they get it back over the net, the next person hits it all the way down to the left. They'll all run down *there*. Sooner or later, they'll get tired out, and we'll win. They'll all be in one big clump, and they'll get tired, they'll run all over each other, they'll get winded from all those Camels they smoke, and we'll beat them."

Meds were kicking in. We didn't believe her, but the idea of winning at anything after so much loss and confusion was charming enough to send us to bed happy. Happy—450 milligrams of Elavil kind of happy.

Later, when I told my internist in the real world how much Elavil I was taking, he gasped. He just didn't believe me.

The next morning, she had to explain it all to us again. It made sense. We weren't athletic, we weren't strong, except for the glass-room kid, but we were smarter than the redneck bikers. Smart enough not to get a tattoo or arrested for dealing cocaine to some undercover cop and sent to rehab to avoid hard time.

We played it her way. We hit the ball to the extreme edges of the court, over and over again, and they trampled all over themselves trying to get to it, leaving the other end completely unguarded. It was like a human demolition derby.

We beat them, and boy did it make them mad. We beat them again, and they started to get a really nasty look in their eyes, but before anything ugly could happen gym time was over for the day. We had done as we were told; even the glass-room kid had stood solidly in one of the front squares and sent the ball flying down to the left-side boundary.

We had beaten them, and we never lost to them again.

There was, of course, more defeat than victory in our collective story. There was more tragedy than triumph. Once I got out, I never went back there—it's not the kind of place you go for some casual sightseeing—and I don't know what happened to those people once I had spent my three weeks with them.

Maybe the psychiatrist did die. She probably did. People who want to generally do. Maybe the glass-room kid never came out of whatever it was that had put him so deep in the well. Maybe he saw the stars from the deep darkness down there. Personally, anhedonia, I have found, is not a passing phase.

I heard this old country guy say once, "I think you decide pretty early on how happy you're going to be, and then you just go on and be it." But I don't think that's the case for a lot of people. For a lot of people, for a lot of the people I met in the bin, I think personal choice has very little to do with it.

There was so much we had done to ourselves, so much we said in our sessions that our hearts were rent with sorrow. There is so much that happens to the human heart that is in the realm of the unthinkable, the unknowable, the unbearable.

How most people carry on is a mystery. What they talk about at supper. How they can stand to sit in front of a TV from eight until Leno every night. How they can think bowling is fun. How they choose their neckties. How they bear the weight of everyday life without screaming. How a person can go through a whole life and never once contemplate suicide, like people who have never once wanted to be a movie star. How one young man can be handsome and strong and marry an heiress and work at Debevoise and Plimpton and retire to Nantucket to await the visits of his grandchildren, how they can be sailing in the bay while another young man, exactly like the first, can end up in a glass room in Lexington, Kentucky, on Haldol and Thorazine, without hope, without a girlfriend, without a future, and how easily the one can become the other. How one woman can take Gatorade to every one of her son's lacrosse games and another can lie in bed all day weeping, popping generic drugs, watching *Oprah* as though waiting for the Second Coming, and piling her dirty dishes in the laundry room. How life goes in bad directions when your heart is asleep.

It's a mystery, and there is no answer. But we beat them at volleyball. It didn't make anything better. It didn't change the course of our lives or keep bad things from happening, even the very same things that had happened before.

But we beat them at volleyball.

The Summer of Our Suicides

On my thirty-fifth birthday, August 4, 1983, I had dinner in a charming restaurant called Devon House with four women I liked. Then I went home, got in bed with the light on, and did what I had planned to do for a year.

On the morning of my previous birthday, I had awakened to the mess of my life and thought, If things don't get better in a year, I'm going to kill myself.

The year had passed. I slit my wrist.

I didn't weep. I didn't think of anybody I knew. I didn't think of revenge or feel remorse. I slit my left wrist with my right hand. I'm right-handed.

The skin gave easily, and the blood flowed down my arm into my cupped hand and onto the sheets. The pain was searing.

I could see my room in minute detail, the desk, the scattered papers, the phone, the dirty clothes thrown on the Thonet chair. I could see the pictures of my mother and father in their tarnished silver frames. I could see the building across the street through the dirty windows, through the orange glow of the street lamp. I could hear the rattle of the cheap air conditioner.

The blood was a rich red, redder than I had thought. It was

a beautiful color. Crimson. Like the dark glossy lipstick of a beautiful woman. It glistened wet in the light. I was in love with my blood. The skin of my left arm was white and milky and pure, snow nobody had walked on. The cut widened, and I could see the meat beneath my own flesh.

This is it, I thought. Nobody can say this is a rash decision. I've thought about nothing else for a year. I've waited long enough. This is what I've waited for all my life.

It didn't feel tragic. It felt brilliantly mesmerizing. It felt astute.

I had written notes. To my parents. To my lovely sister. I had, of course, said it was nobody's fault. The notes were lyrical and winsome. One note was written to a friend of mine. He had once given me two thousand dollars in cash when I had no money. I was so poor, I had to walk to his apartment to get it. Nothing in the bank. No credit, nothing left on my credit cards. I had seven cents left in the world. Seven pennies. He gave me twenty one-hundred-dollar bills.

He had been a bartender when he was young, and he once said to me that the only real money was cash money.

Earlier in the summer, he had tried to kill himself, but that wasn't the reason. That wasn't at all why I did what I did. His story was altogether different. There is no suicide except your own. The rest is just sad and terrible stuff that happens to some-body else.

He was a bookie, a bookie who could quote the sonnets of Shakespeare, who loved the theater but would only go alone and sit on the aisle because he hated crowds, a bookie who drank more than a case of Heineken a day, so many that his wife kept the empties in the downstairs bathtub until the boy could come take them back to the store. He was a bookie who had a secret life, led late at night. Drug dealers and bars and after-hours clubs where gay boys danced with their shirts off. His wife didn't know where he was half the time.

He was a bookie who was generous beyond belief with the amazing amounts of cash he carried with him at all times. His wife was beautiful, a model, and he had a one-year-old baby.

He didn't find killing himself an easy thing to do. He had a generous and forgiving nature. He tried once and couldn't go through with it. His kindness and intelligence argued against it, but when he did it two days later, he did it with a precision and a viciousness that was astonishing.

I talked to him on the phone the night before he did it. He sounded fine.

He got into his green Mercedes on a warm summer afternoon and drove from his apartment on Beekman Place to Connecticut, where he checked into a cheap motel. He went out that night, to a restaurant that happened, he noticed when he looked at the menu, to have the same name as his baby daughter. He couldn't eat. Then he went back to the motel.

He was a big man, and like a lot of big men in the summer, he was always hot. Before he went to bed, he turned the air conditioner to its highest setting, so the room would be cold enough.

When he woke up, he got dressed in a pair of khaki pants, a clean white shirt, and a Bill Blass blazer with gold buttons. Then he took out a razor blade and cut his wrist so deeply he severed the nerves. Then he took the razor and slit his other arm from the elbow to the wrist. He had left no note. Not a word.

He hit an artery. He bled profusely. He bled on the bed and the cheap thin rug and the bathroom tile; he bled until he fainted. Ah, this is it, he thought. This is the end.

Then he woke up. He was dizzy, and he was still bleeding, but he was alive. He took the razor and cut his wrists again, and he bled and passed out again, thinking, Ah, this is it, and then he woke up again. So he took the razor and he slit his throat. There was blood everywhere. He was bathed in his own blood.

He lost consciousness one more time and one more time he thought, Ah, this is it. But he came to, and he went to the phone, and he called the front desk.

"There's something wrong with the air-conditioning," he said to the desk clerk. "I'm freezing to death." He didn't know what he was saying anymore. He had lost focus.

The maid who found him threw up and fainted. He was still alive. He was conscious. He could talk. The air-conditioning had saved him. The room had been cold enough to slow his circulation, so that, as massive as his injuries were, they had not been enough to kill him. The cold had congealed his blood.

He was stitched together. He was brought back to the city. He was hospitalized. He was near death. Only three people besides his wife knew he had done this. I was one of them. This was in June, right after the Belmont Stakes. It was three days after his daughter's birthday.

The official story was that he had gone to visit his sick father in Georgia. He owed half a million dollars to some really bad people.

The reality was that he was heavily sedated in a locked room in a locked ward at Payne Whitney, under twenty-four-hour-a-day surveillance by burly thugs. I went to see him.

The hospital was like a Victorian nightmare, full of drooling lunatics, slobbering and muttering and screaming. It was dark. It was dirty. It was loud.

His condition was a shock. He had cut himself so deeply that one arm was in a cast. His face was as pale as his hospital pajamas.

His other arm was bandaged to the elbow, his neck was bandaged, and he barely knew where he was. When he spoke, he didn't make sense. It was only later he told me the whole story.

What do you say? What would you say? I was terrified of him. There was no way to make conversation of any kind. I told him I was glad he was alive. I told him he was my best friend, that if I had lost him I would feel bereft for a very long time. You say anything in a situation like that. Anything to pretend it isn't happening. You want to believe it isn't real.

He told me he just couldn't stand the mediocrity of his life anymore. He talked like a man underwater.

"It's not anything else," he said. "It's the mediocrity." He moved in slow motion. He was glazed with sweat and drugs.

The ward was filled with crazy people, schizophrenics, people who had just lost their minds for no reason, men and women whose hearts and spirits were china plates, broken irrevocably, people for whom there was no world outside the doors of the ward, would never be, no sustenance more vital or soothing than the medications they were being given. They went to a special window to get them. The pills were in little paper cups, like lemon ices.

It was a freak show, people in bathrobes shuffling blankly from window to window, a collection of tics. The bookie belonged in the green glow of the warm bar we always went to, telling stories, paying for everybody's drinks with cash, doing cocaine in the bathroom. Giving drugs to whoever wanted them out of the goodness of his heart, and because he always had more of them than anybody.

A few years before, we had sat up all night, running from bar to bar, then to after-hours clubs, ending up in his study, doing drugs until his sleepy wife came and told him to go to bed and told me to leave. It was five o'clock in the morning. Her patience was exhausted.

I was supposed to fly to Virginia early the next morning for Christmas. He said the only way to make an early flight was to stay up all night. We believed that kind of thing back then. It was almost light when I got back to my apartment.

My father met me at the airport. I looked terrible, clean-shaven, perfectly pressed and expensive, loaded with bag after bag of presents from Bergdorf's and Three Lives and Saks, but terrible. I looked like death on a cracker. I told him a friend of mine had tried to kill himself the night before, and I had sat up all night with his wife at the hospital. I was so hungover I would have said anything.

He'd be OK, I said. But it was close. I said he was just sad, and that I couldn't go to a cocktail party I'd been to every year since I was twelve.

Once, at that party, a professor at the college sent a note over to me, written on a cocktail napkin. It said, "I had such hopes for you. When did you get to be so dull? Why are you so ordinary?"

I had sent a note back. On a cocktail napkin. I quoted Eliot. "I am not Prince Hamlet," it said. "Nor was meant to be; / Am an attendant lord, one that will do / to swell a progress, start a scene or two." I was nineteen.

I looked at my wounded, almost-dead friend and felt guilt. As though I had told a lie and caused it.

At first, I thought that he, in his terror and his failure, had saved me from my own suicide, with my birthday less than two months away. I had thought of it for a year. Now I wouldn't have to think of it anymore. That's what I thought.

I went to see him every single day, seven days a week, more than I could stand, and I saw him turn into one of the shuffling zombies. Tranquilizers. Antipsychotics. Anything given to the violent and self-destructive. He couldn't bend the fingers of his left hand where the nerve was severed. The bandage on his neck made him look like he was about to get a haircut. The heat was excruciating.

It was a terrible thing to do, a terrible moment to have endured. To do that to his wife, in whom he delighted, whose charm and humor and jet black hair he took for granted, and to his baby daughter, whom he adored, the sheer desperation of it and the cuts and the endless sad and cruel details of the blue blazer and the khaki pants and the air-conditioning and the bandages and the drugs—these were all strong reasons to avoid the same fate.

But that feeling only lasted for a few weeks. I began to see what he had done as a necessary action that opened the door for me, a vision of my own way out, a harbinger, even if he had failed.

Even if he had failed, he had made his point. He had written his point in blood on his clothes and his body and the walls and floors and bed linens of a motel room in Connecticut. And I had no wife. I had no lovely daughter. It seemed, at the time, that I had no one in all the world.

He started shock therapy. In his six months in the hospital, he had something like thirty-seven treatments. He began to look forward to them, because they rendered him speechless and thoughtless for two days, and the blank hours were the hours he found the most bearable. He became addicted to the electricity shooting through his brain.

Nowadays, you can have it done in an office visit. They don't call it shock therapy anymore. They call it electroconvulsive therapy. ECT. Much more modern. Stigma-free.

Psychiatrists tell you how easy it is. It's a walk in the park. People, even famous people, talk about it on television talk shows. They say how much better they feel, how much more cheerful, how it's changed their lives. Anything's possible now, they say.

It wasn't that way then. After a month in the hospital, he was not merely depressed; he was crazy. Every day, I could watch him slip farther into a madness that wrapped him like a wet sheet.

He began to carry a small ball of Silly Putty. He was never without it, and he would form it into endless shapes. He called it his worry fairy, and when he slept, he stuck it on the wall by his bed. When he had his electroshock treatments, he clutched it in his hand.

I began to carry a razor blade. I got a dozen single-edged blades from the art studio of the advertising agency where I worked, the kind used for cutting mat board. I was embarrassed and scared even to ask for them. In the art studio, I thought they would know what I was going to do with them.

I carried one with me all the time. The same one. If I didn't have it, I panicked. I carried it in my pants pocket, and I was always glad to be wearing a pair of pants that had one of those little watch pockets at the waist, or a coin pocket in the larger right-hand pocket. I called these razor pants. I slept with a razor in my hand.

I would find it in the bed next to me when I woke up. One night, I lost the blade while I slept. I looked everywhere. I never found it. I had to choose another one.

I carried it when I went to see the bookie in the hospital. I never told anybody. I tried to make conversation with him. I tried to get close to the terror and the madness and the mystery of the act itself, but it was beyond comprehension. I turned the blade in my hand as I talked to him, as I tried to nurse him back to sanity with compassion and kindness.

The razor blade I carried had a protective cardboard wrapping around it, so the sharp edge of the blade was covered. It was held shut by glue. I decided, as the cardboard got dirtier, stained by sweat and ink from my fingers, that when the cardboard came off the blade on its own, I would cut my wrists open.

Things began to take on a magical quality. Everything was a sign. I saw the world and my friends with a tenderness I had never imagined. Their lives were so beautiful and filled with work and love and ideas and longing, and I loved them in their flesh, in their reality in a world that was becoming more dream-like by the minute. The closer I got to my own death, the more

I loved the world I would no longer be a part of, its startling moments of quietude and beauty, moments that seemed to belong only to other people.

I had never been a part of it, really. The rewards of everyday life, the job well done, the loves explored and lost with bitterness or regret, the loves that expanded into an eternity, the waking up next to the skin of somebody you desired with all your heart, the simple brushing of your hair or the taste of beer, had all seemed to me like things that were happening to other people. I wasn't real in the way they were. I envied them their acceptance, and their assurance.

I had wanted to die since I was twelve.

I wasn't safe. I wasn't permanent. My life was a fiction I had created, like an alien who comes to earth and tries to pass as human. The affections of my friends meant nothing to me, directed, as they were, toward a person who wasn't there. There was nobody home.

I lived alone. I had always felt alone, isolated from real people, even when I was involved in one of my failed love affairs, affairs that failed through my own lassitude, through the desultory small cruelties of the people, men and women, I had chosen to love. My love for them was real. Their love for me was both a myth and a torture and so I wrecked everything. I hurt them, and I left them hurting.

I had started to drink heavily when I was thirty-one. Liquor gave me the ability to endure the company of others, to endure the burden of my own self. I was going through the end of two affairs I had carried on simultaneously, one with a woman with the most beautiful hands, the other with a man who was married.

The first time I saw the woman, at a dinner party in Philadel-phia where she lived, a party given by my lover and his wife, she made a particular gesture with her beautiful hands, holding up her left hand as though she were holding an egg to the light, and I was thunderstruck. She had a small tattoo at the soft part of her hand between the thumb and her first finger, and as she held up the egg, a small bird rose in the air.

On our first date, she came up on the train and we went to the ballet, the first time I had ever been, and we saw *Serenade,* the Bal-anchine masterpiece. The curtain rose, and there stood two dozen women in long tulle skirts, their arms raised, their hands making the same gesture. The gesture she had made at the dinner party. I had never seen anything so beautiful. I knew I loved her.

The first time we had had sex, after the ballet, she had said to me, "Either this leads to my having a baby in two years, or I want to stop right now." I had said, "We'll see." A week later, she had moved to New York from Philadelphia and found a loft near NYU and we were living together. I felt like I was living some-body else's life.

She said once, "You always want to know the end of the story before the story's even started."

She said, "You don't win arguments because you're right. You win because you argue better."

I said, "What happens to us every day is what we'll remem-ber when we are old. Don't you understand that?"

We had a lot of fights. She hated all my friends. She hated my family. She hated the idea of my family.

A friend of hers who slept on the floor of her loft several times when I was there for the night, having sex with her at the other end of the loft, told me two years later, "I always hated you, not just because you suffer fools gladly. You suffer fools *too* gladly." He was from Philadelphia, too. He worked in the garment business. We met for drinks in a hotel so he could tell me this.

After a year, we broke up. After a month, we got back together again. The sex was fantastic. She said so. I lived for it.

The man I had been seeing for five years. We met in Greece, and I knew the first time I saw him that we would be sleeping together, that we would have sex before the summer was over. He was dark, handsome, a photographer. I loved him as I have never loved anybody. The memory of a night when I came back to my white house on Páros and found him waiting on the steps, waiting for me with those eyes in the dark, it pierces my heart.

I loved the first touch of his body as we embraced, the first brush of his chest on my skin. I loved the secrecy of our affair. I loved the darkness of his eyes, his small, pretty hands, his thick legs, the hair that covered his chest and stomach. There was something masculine and feminine about him at the same time. I loved every part of him.

We would get into bed in our underclothes, as though we weren't really going to have sex. Only once, years later, did I pull back the covers to find him naked and waiting. I was touched.

We would make love in the calm waters of the Aegean. He took pictures of my torso. In the photographs, I look so thin, the way young men do.

He was married to a nice woman. I knew her. She was a painter. She once said to me, "I think he's happier since he's known you. I hope you *are* sleeping together." She was sitting in my kitchen in Greece when she said it, and I had nothing to say in return. I figured my silence was a confession, that she knew and accepted the truth. Like *Jules et Jim* through the looking glass.

I wasn't the first man he'd slept with since they had been married. Years later, while they were divorcing, I thought, well, of course she knew.

He once said to me, standing by my bed in his clothes, in Greece, ready to climb the hill in the twilight to his wife and his dinner, while I lay naked under the sheets, twenty-four years old, "One day you'll need me. One day you'll call me in the night and tell me that you need me. And I won't come. I want you to understand that." So I knew the rules. It's not that I didn't know the rules. I kissed him, and he went home.

I didn't know what they wanted of me, either of them. My lovers. I didn't know who they thought I was. I was ugly and fatal. They must have seen that. But I know this: During the time I was sleeping with them both, I was happier than I've ever been.

When I made love to him, I was making love to the body I wanted to have. When I had sex with her, I was loving the masculine part of myself, like making love to a man through her body, and I loved my ability to give them both pleasure, one shy and secretive, the other passionate and public.

Once, I made love to her without taking off my watch. When I put my hands up along her face, the way men do in the movies when they kiss women, cradling their cheeks in their hands, I could hear the ticking. She said, "I knew you'd leave your watch on."

She was a photographer, too. She took my picture naked, on my thirtieth birthday. It was midnight. I was aroused by being looked at, by being seen by the lens, by her piercing eye. That split second would always be there. I would be naked forever. In the photograph, my hair is still wet from the bath.

I loved the fact that I could have both halves of what I wanted. I loved the fact that my desire had found its full expression. I loved kissing them on the mouth, the taste of their tongues. I think kissing is what separates us from the animals and makes us divine.

I loved going from one to the other. He knew about her and was glad. She knew nothing about him.

Both affairs ended almost simultaneously. She and I broke up on a plane on the way back from a trip to Europe, a trip when she had behaved more and more badly, her fears that I didn't love her, that I didn't love her enough, ruining Paris, ruining London, causing me to stop every day at the flower market, until our room at the hotel looked like a lavish funeral parlor.

Her father had abandoned her as a child. She had watched him leave on a train. He had been handsome. She had dated a handsome man before she met me. She was afraid everyone would leave her.

"We're turning into the kind of people I don't want to be," I told her, and then I left. She had been right. I abandoned her without giving her a baby. We had been dating for two years. I was her worst nightmare come true.

A month later, she called me up and told me I owed her a hundred dollars. She was rich and didn't need it. I went to see her and paid her the money. We went to a hamburger joint on the Bowery, where I had a beer in the middle of the afternoon. She said to me, "You drink all the time now."

That was the end of her story. I have seen her twice since then, on the street. We didn't speak.

His wife found out he was having an affair with a man in Greece, cheating both her and me, and she asked him if he had slept with me and he said yes, and I got dragged into it, and I didn't want to be dragged into it, and so I shut him out of my life. I was drinking wine when I told him to leave me alone. He said, "Don't open another bottle for me," but I opened one anyway, and then he left.

I have never stopped regretting it.

Then I stayed home in my filthy fifth-floor walkup in a bad neighborhood. I painted the whole apartment battleship gray, like a prison cell. I drank a liter of gin a day. And never once, since then, have I waked up to say good morning to another human being in my bed. Never once, since then, have I kissed someone goodnight. I have built around myself a wall of sexual invisibility, and the desires of my body, real and voracious, have grown totally separate from the desires of my heart, ephemeral and essentially kind.

I discovered anonymous sex, the desires of the pure body, the starvation of the heart. Sucking, kissing, fucking in the dark, in tiny, lonely rooms. I don't know how I knew where to go, but I did, and I prowled the night like a panther, high on gin and cocaine. There were places you could go, then. The men always said something nice when it was over. And there was always liquor and cocaine and poppers.

Somebody once said to me that the rise in cocaine usage exactly matched the introduction of the cash machine, because suddenly, as long as you had an ATM card and a hundred dollars, you were good to go, twenty-four hours a day. Sometimes it was light out when I came home. After three years, I knew it was time to kill myself.

After the bookie had been in the hospital a month, as my birthday was getting closer and closer, I began to have hallucinations, or rather, I began to have a single recurring hallucination. Every day, as I sat in meetings at work, starched and attentive, as I sat with my friend in the horror show that was his daily life in the insane asylum, as I knelt in prayer in church or sat in Yankee Stadium, this chimera would lunge at me again and again.

The thin cardboard was getting looser on the razor, filthy from the oil on the tips of my fingers. My best friend was in an electrified haze with the worry fairy. There was no one to tell.

I could see with absolute clarity the underside of my arm, the white skin, the fine blue veins. I could see two fingers, the thumb and the first finger of my hand, spreading the skin taut. I could see the razor slice into the skin and watch the blood begin to spurt and flow. It wasn't until years later that I realized there were three hands involved in the hallucination. One arm to slice open, one hand to spread the skin taut, one hand to hold the razor. It wasn't until then I realized who the third hand belonged to.

I knew it was crazy. I knew I had to tell somebody. I was having sex with strangers. I was drinking and doing more cocaine than I could afford. I was going to slit my wrist open. I was going to die. And my birthday was a week away.

On the morning of my birthday, I saw a psychiatrist. I told him I was going to kill myself and I told him why.

"When?" he asked.

"Today," I said. His gaze didn't waver.

We talked for an hour. He told me mine was not a psychiatric dilemma but a spiritual one. He was a Jungian. Then he made an appointment for the next week and I went to work. In the afternoon, I reached into my pocket, and the paper had come loose from the razor. It was time. Then I went to the charming dinner and excused myself the minute the last bite of food was eaten and then I took a taxicab home and got into bed and slit my wrist.

I made a phone call. To one of the charming women. But when she answered, I didn't speak. I couldn't think of what to say. I hung up the phone and bled gently for an hour. The blood glittered on my skin, like red, sparkling Christmas lights. Then I got up, stopped the bleeding, put bandages on my arm, and went to sleep, the razor on the table by my bed, the blood now a thick brown coating on the edge. And then I got up and went to work.

The next night I did it again, more fiercely. And the next and the next. I stopped in the drugstore and bought gauze pads and gauze wrapping and every kind of bandage I could find that would cover a large area, feeling like a criminal, sure they would divine my insane secret. I still went to see my friend and the worry fairy every day, and then I went out to dinner and drank as much as possible. When the bill came, I was embarrassed to see the hatch marks indicating the number of drinks I had had. Eight. Ten. I got up the minute dinner was eaten and went home and slit my wrist. The whole area between my left wrist and my elbow was covered with deep cuts. I had to take off the bandages to get to the skin, and often the gauze stuck to the old cuts and they started to bleed again and always they hurt. They stung like fire.

But the cutting didn't hurt, and the hallucination had stopped. I would lie on my sofa in my undershorts in the August heat and cut my skin open and smear the blood all over my chest and my arms, until the hair was matted to my skin and the blood dried and began to crack. Like those mud people.

There was an erotic pleasure in the cutting. I wept as I did it, and there was an erotic pleasure in that as well.

I saw the psychiatrist again. I told him I had cut myself deeply and repeatedly, and he never even asked me to roll up my sleeves. He didn't want proof. I never saw him again. I never paid his bill.

The bookie and the worry fairy got out for the weekend, to see if he could stand the real world again. At that point, he had had sixteen electroshock treatments. He and his wife gave me a beautiful pair of antique gold cuff links as a present for being so faithful to him.

We went to their country house for the weekend, a small house near the sea. I was helping in the kitchen and reached for a salad bowl and the bandage slipped up my arm and she saw the first deep cuts on my wrist, the hard dried blood in the wound.

"Oh, you boys," was all she said. Oh, you boys.

He couldn't stand the outside world. He felt unsafe. He missed the electroshock. They had no health insurance, but he went back to the hospital, kissing his daughter farewell. I went back to cutting.

I did it everywhere. I did it in taxis. I did it in the men's room at restaurants. The same monotony of composure and pain, the trip to the hospital, the dinner with friends, the dash home to the razor.

I felt, every time, the release of some pressure that was pressing on my heart. I felt free. I felt I was home, after a long time away.

One night, I had dinner at Orso with my oldest friend in New York, and, after dinner, she suggested we sneak into the second act of *Dreamgirls,* the Broadway musical. We were at the age when that kind of thing was fun. We sneaked in and found two seats on the aisle. The curtain rose, I excused myself, and went downstairs to the men's room and slit my arm. I bandaged it with toilet paper. Then I returned to my seat, to the slightest glance from my friend, and watched the second act of a musical based on the career of the Supremes, the sixties singing group.

In the cab on the way to drop her off, I had to hold my arm upright, so the blood wouldn't drip onto the floor of the cab. We stopped for a nightcap, and I could feel the blood pooling in my elbow and the lining of my jacket.

One night, I cut myself so deeply I needed to go to the emergency room. The cuts were getting longer and deeper and more vicious. I stood at the door, one bloody hand on the doorknob, almost fainting, and I couldn't go to the hospital. They would make me stay. They would give me electroshock treatments. I would have a worry fairy of my own. So I sat up until dawn with ice packs on the wound, making the blood stop, and then I dressed and went to work.

At lunch, I was eating a hamburger with a guy I worked with, when I looked down and noticed there were bloodstains all over my white shirtsleeve. He didn't seem to notice. My arm was still bleeding from the night before.

I jumped up and put on my jacket and ran out, saying I would be back. I went home and changed my shirt again, rebandaging the wound, and went to the emergency room. It was like being on Mars. I forgot why I was there. I didn't know how to pay. I had left my credit cards at home; I had very little cash. I knew they would make me stay. I thought they would call the police. I hung at the doorway, terrified of any alternative I could imagine, and then I went back home and put on ice and finally more bandages, a new shirt, my arm thick with gauze, and went back to work. I had been away for three hours. Nobody said anything.

My left arm was full. My left arm was hamburger. I started on my right arm, the thrill of fresh skin. My arms were a crochet of wounds. A spiderweb of blood. My apartment had blood on the furniture, on the walls, on the door handles. I hadn't cleaned it in weeks. Mice sniffed at the blood on the floor. Blood doesn't come out of wood. Blood leaves dark brown stains.

It went on for two months. The thrill of the cutting never ceased for a second. The pain was excruciating during the day. The secrecy was my deepest joy.

When you're lying on your sofa cutting open your own skin, life becomes very vivid. There is a vivacity you've never known before. And you'll never know it again.

A friend later told me that, all that summer, after the many dinners when I would rush into the night, she thought I was an addict. I was.

My friends meant nothing to me. Work meant less than nothing. The dozens of shirts I threw away, my beautiful cotton and linen shirts, meant nothing. Eloquence and sex and the pleasures of the world were hollow. The feel of hot blood on the warm late summer nights, alone in my derelict apartment, was all there was.

In September, I was called for jury duty, to start the fourth of October. I could see the irony of being put in a position to sit in judgment on others.

Then an extraordinary thing happened. I was sitting on my sofa, red blood draining into the cheap red cotton upholstery, and the phone rang. It was an old friend, a woman called Doc who lived in Lexington, Kentucky. She actually was a doctor. She was a psychotherapist. She treated rich Kentucky neurotics.

She asked me how I was and what was going on. I told her. I told her in detail. I was thickly bandaged on both arms from the wrist to the elbow. The telephone was spackled with blood. My two dear lovers were long gone.

I was cutting myself, I told her. I couldn't stop. The blood seeped through the bandages, no matter how careful I was. The blood clotted into the gauze.

"Honey," she said. "This does not sound good. This does not sound *good*, sugar. At all."

She told me I needed to be in a hospital. She told me I needed to come to the South to be in a hospital, that Yankees had no conception of the deep sorrows that Southerners felt, and couldn't do a thing about it.

"Leave it to me," she said. "Just get here. I'll get you into the hospital here. They'll take good care of you. I know the head psychiatrist. He's not one of these bullshit guys." Her slow whiskey drawl was as warm and comforting as the laying on of hands.

"And don't hurt yourself anymore. It's not getting you anywhere."

I hung up the phone and cut my right arm just below the elbow.

The next day I got an airplane ticket. I kept insisting on the phone that I wanted a direct flight, not knowing a direct flight was different from a nonstop flight. And I realized something. I didn't know what people wore in mental hospitals, but I imagined that merino wool double-pleated knife-creased trousers didn't figure highly. So I went to Bloomingdale's and bought sweatshirts and khakis and T-shirts, as though I were packing to go to camp.

I picked up my ticket. I would have to change in Pittsburgh.

I went to the hospital to say good-bye. I tried to explain I was going away. I tried to explain it wasn't his fault, although he had no idea what I was talking about. I said that the machinery had been set in motion long before he drove to Connecticut, but I don't think he heard any of it.

His doctor stopped in for a visit, to see how the latest electroshock had gone. I was sitting in a hospital armchair, and there was blood dripping from the ends of my fingers onto the linoleum floor. Nobody noticed.

On the morning of October 4, I went into work early and went in to see my boss, a man who smoked cigars at seven-forty-five in the morning.

"I know I'm supposed to go to jury duty this morning. I just . . . I just wanted you to know I'm not going. I'm going away, probably for three weeks. I'm going to a mental hospital. I don't feel well." It was probably the only piece of bad news he ever took with grace.

In the airport in Pittsburgh, as I walked the long way from gate to gate, blood ran down my arm and dripped onto my suitcase. Nobody noticed.

Doc and I sat over drinks that night, at her house. I showed her my arms. We talked quietly. I slept in her guest room and the next morning, she dropped me at the door of the hospital.

I stared at the doors. I was homesick already. I was homesick for the blade and the booze. I was homesick for the men in the tiny dark rooms who always said thank you, who always said something nice. About my body. About my greedy kiss. I was, most of all, homesick for the blood in the golden light from the street lamps, and the pain that shot up my arm like the venom from a snake.

My insurance paid for most of the stay. It had never occurred to me that I would have to carry some of the cost. I paid for the rest with a credit card. A Visa card. It took years to pay it off.

I had my razor blade in my pocket, but I knew. It was over. Just like that, with one phone call, it had ended, one touch to the heart, one voice that got through the haze, one word that saved my life. It was over.

I was a curiosity in the hospital. I had come all the way from New York. The mental hospital was in a town that had the same name as the town I grew up in. The irony didn't escape me.

My brother flew up from Atlanta to spend the day with me. Sweet. The psychiatrist allowed me to go out to lunch. The world was very loud. I told my brother the doctor thought it would be good for me to discuss in detail what had happened to me. My brother said he'd rather not know. It was kind of him to come, anyway.

My mother called. You don't just disappear for three weeks. I stood at a pay phone in the hall. "What did you do?" she asked, accusing me as though I had committed a felony and was serving time for, say, assault with a deadly weapon. Which, of course, I was, sort of. It was the only time I ever cried in the hospital.

I stayed for three weeks. After that my doctor thought it was best to confront my life in my own context. I was being sent home, high on Elavil.

When I left, the kind doctor told me to stay away from Tanqueray, and to stay away from my apartment. I didn't do either one.

The scars were thick and purple, but over the years, they've turned thin and white. You can barely see them, except in the summer when I get tan, and then they rise to the surface, like lace on my skin. Nobody in my family has ever asked me why I went to the loony bin. My niece, once, looking at the still-purple scars, asked me with shock what had happened to me. I told her I'd had an accident; I'd gone through a plateglass window. With both arms. Nobody ever asked again.

I still carry a razor blade with me at all times. It is always in my pocket. Two weeks ago, I cut myself again, like a drunk taking a drink after twenty years.

It hurt like hell.

Butter Day

The thing about Butter Day was you had to bring your own cream. Every child brought a pint of heavy cream on Butter Day and we couldn't have been happier about it.

In kindergarten and first grade, we went to a little one-woman private school and we had many little festivals and ceremonies to break up the monotony of learning how to read and add and subtract, but Butter Day just about took the cake. It didn't come on any particular day—it came when Mrs. Lackman wanted it to come—and so it was more sort of like the first snowfall or a hurricane than, say, Washington's Birthday, which we elaborately celebrated. She would just, one day, tell us all to tell our mothers that we needed to bring a pint of cream, heavy whipping cream, the next day, and we would know it was on.

Of course, as kindergartners, we had no idea what was coming, but, by the time we were in first grade, when we heard the word *cream,* we knew. We just knew, because we'd already been through it once, unlike the babies in the other room.

The kindergartners sat on little chairs in one room, and the first graders sat at long tables in the other room, and Mrs. Lackman was presumably supposed to wander back and forth, supervising both classes, but I got the feeling she didn't really like the first graders anymore, so they were left largely unattended.

When I was in kindergarten, one of my classmates was a lit-tle red-haired boy who was the son of the farmer who lived next door to us, although that's sort of misleading since there were ten acres separating our doors, but they were our closest neigh-bors. Every morning, he would stand at the end of their drive-way and my father would pick him up and take us to school.

He was a funny kid, charming actually. But he had problems right away. Serious problems.

When you needed to go to the bathroom at Mrs. Lackman's, you were supposed to hold up one finger if you had to pee, and two fingers if you had to do the Unspeakable Other. It was maybe the second day of school when he had to go to the bath-room, at eleven o'clock, and he held up one finger, but Mrs. Lackman avoided him and went on going over the alphabet. He violently waved his finger, but there was no way he was going to get her attention. She was moving through the alphabet like a freight train, and he just wasn't part of her plan at all.

He peed in his pants. He peed in his pants and it dribbled on the floor, making noise, a wet noise like a tiny waterfall or a gut-ter spout after the rain has stopped, and Mrs. Lackman paused and looked at him and said to the whole class, "Now, class, look at what a little baby we have! Such a baby he can't even control himself. Don't we just hate babies? Aren't we glad to be grown up enough that we can follow the rules and not be babies any-more?" It went on for a long time, but it was just more of the same, Mrs. Lackman walking up to him and looking at the small puddle on the hardwood floor.

"Hey, first graders! Come look at what a little baby we have today," and him just sitting there in his wet shorts, his face as red as his hair.

The next day, she'd brought in a high chair and put it in the middle of the room. She made him sit in it because he was such a baby and babies needed to be put in high chairs. At exactly eleven o'clock, he held up one finger while she was making us do our counting or something, and again she completely avoided him and, once again, he peed on the floor. Except now he was in a high chair and the pee had farther to fall so the sound was even louder.

Every day it was the same. Every day she viciously infantilized him, every day she refused to let him go to the bathroom, and every day he peed on the floor.

It was no wonder he didn't come back for first grade. It was no wonder he became a major felon later in life, doing hard time in the state pen for dealing hard drugs to crystal meth–loving rednecks. Who wouldn't turn into a sociopathic drug-dealing hard timer after going through that at the age of five? But he was lucky. His wife stuck by him and he got over it and now he has a successful excavation business.

My sister, when she was in the first grade, in the unsupervised first grade, suddenly felt one day that she had to throw up. She panicked. She didn't want to throw up on her long table, but she didn't know how many fingers to hold up.

She went to the door of the kindergarten class and held up one finger but Mrs. Lackman shook her head. She went back to her table, but she was feeling worse, and so she went to the door and held up two fingers with what she hoped was a sense of urgency, a sense of immediate need. Mrs. Lackman wouldn't even look at her.

She went back to her table, but she was getting closer and

closer to vomiting, so she got up and ran to the door and held up an unprecedented three fingers, not knowing what else to do, a sure signal of imminent danger, she felt, but Mrs. Lackman looked at her like she was a visitor from Mars or somewhere so she went back to her table and threw up all over Johnny Sheridan, the one boy in her class she thought was really, really cute. Their relationship never recovered to the degree she had hoped.

Later in life, of course, that sort of thing can be gotten over. There is a time you can throw up on your date and get away with it. You can even laugh about it. I did it once in Baltimore after an opening at the Baltimore Museum of Art and we went on with our romance uninterrupted. And she was my French teacher. But this is not the way it is in the first grade.

So, although we were carefully schooled from day one in the one- and two-finger principle, it almost never applied to daily life or even to urgent needs. Mrs. Lackman ran a tight ship. Apparently the natural functions of five- and six-year-olds played no part in it.

My brother had already been through Mrs. Lackman's, where he distinguished himself with his total brilliance. When he came home from his first day there, he told my mother he wasn't going to school anymore. She asked him why and he said he didn't want to.

She said, "But think of everything you'll miss. You'll learn to add and subtract, you'll learn to read so we won't have to read to you anymore and—"

"I already learned to read," he said sullenly.

"When?" my mother asked.

"I learned to read today." And then he sat down and proceeded to read anything she threw at him, Dick and Jane books, the *Richmond Times-Dispatch* sports section, anything. He was a sly one.

He was the kind of person who wouldn't show the slightest interest in a thing until he had mentally perfected it and had only to begin doing it for real. Take talking, for instance. He didn't talk until he was three. It drove my parents wild. They kept trying to make him say *wa-wa* like Helen Keller, to say *dada* or *wee-wee*, but he just refused to utter a sound, not a peep. They took him to a doctor. They had his hearing tested. They did everything parents could do with a child who went through every day mute as a rock.

Then one day he was sitting down in his high chair or whatever having some soup for lunch, and he looked at my mother and he said to her, clear as a bell, "I want a cracker." So when he said he'd learned to read in one day, what he meant was that he'd figured it out a long time ago and he'd been reading things over in his mind, practicing on the sly when people thought they were reading to him. He didn't mean he'd learned to read. He meant he was *ready* to read, he felt the need to go public with the reading thing, the way he'd only spoken because he wanted a cracker to go with his soup. He'd been *able* to talk all along.

He used to concentrate so hard he'd curl his tongue between his teeth, and once in a football game, he got hit in the jaw and he came damn close to biting it off. He had to have stitches in his tongue. He was just very concentrated.

Mrs. Lackman had a son who was a youthful schizophrenic.

He was certifiable, as we say. Certified to do what I've never been sure. To go to the crazy house at Western State, I guess.

I'm not sure how old he was, but he was a lot older, maybe eighteen. One day when he was off his medication, he got stopped by the police with a briefcase full of, as it turned out, elaborate plans and explosives to blow up the university. After that, he was barred from ever going on the campus, and, in fact, he still can't go there today. He was a dark-haired boy with sparkling eyes, and he used to lurk in the doorways between the kindergarten and the first grade until his mother told him to go upstairs and mind his own business, presumably as long as his business didn't involve blowing up public buildings with significant numbers of people inside them.

When he was on his medication, he was gentle as a lamb. He would have let anybody go to the bathroom, even for number two. He would never have made a five-year-old sit in a baby's high chair.

It's a wonder we ever learned to read at all what with getting ready for the pageants. There was a really big pageant on Washington's Birthday, and then there was another really big pageant on May Day.

The Washington's Birthday pageant was more of a torture than May Day, because it was a play and everybody had a part to play and you had to memorize dialogue and you had to memorize it perfectly or you just knew it was going to be worse for you than even peeing on the floor would have been.

I never got to play George Washington. This one boy got all the good parts because he was already as big as a truck driver, strong and athletic and good-looking, and he had the biggest head in the class, which was, for some reason, vital to all the lead parts, both male and female. He was every mother's dream son, he went on to be captain of the football team and homecoming king, and every kind of social reward that could be bestowed came his way from the age of five, and he was a nice guy besides, so nobody had to feel bad about it. It was just naturally going to be him who got to play the Father of Our Country.

My father was dragged into it one year. He had to stand up in front of all the parents of the other children, with many of whom he regularly sat down to cocktails, and recite a really mawkish speech that began, "I am the flag," and concluded with the Pledge of Allegiance, where at least we all joined in.

It was the one time I was ever proud of my father. I forgot for a minute that he made my skin crawl. I forgot while he spoke how afraid he made me feel. The hard, metallic distaste went away, just for that brief time when he was being so bravely humiliated, and I saw him as others must have seen him, handsome and tall and straight as a flagpole.

People now tell me I look like him. I don't. I hope I don't.

There was the scene with the cherry tree, of course, and crossing the Delaware, and being sworn in as our first president, but the truly startling scene was the scene that depicted George Washington's birth.

Mrs. Lackman had written every word of the pageant herself. None of it came out of a book.

There was Mr. Washington outside the door, pacing and churning his hands together, frantic with worry, and there was Mrs. Washington in a big cardboard bed giving birth.

And then there was Mammy. It was Mammy who delivered

the play's classic line, its moment of ultimate drama. She picked up the little rubber doll that had been wrapped in swaddling clothes so you could just barely see its little rubber face, and she brought out the baby to show it off, and this is what she said, in a high voice like Butterfly McQueen: "Lawzy, Miz Washin'ton, you got a fiiiine baby boy. He look lak he a monf ole awready."

Needless to say, there were no little black children holding up one finger or two at Mrs. Lackman's, no proud black faces beaming from the parents' section. God, when you think of it, it's a miracle we didn't all grow up to bomb public buildings or deal cocaine for a living.

May Day was another story. Of course, the boy who got to play Washington also got to be King of the May, probably two years running. Who got to be the Queen of the May escapes me. I'm sure she was lovely. And big-headed. I have noticed, in my brief encounters, that celebrities tend to have bigger heads than your average people, so maybe this was Mrs. Lackman's way of putting in an early bid for fame for her beloveds.

Once, for instance, I had dinner with Elizabeth Taylor. She had the biggest head I've ever seen on a human being, even though she was quite small. Tiny feet. She looked, from the rear, like a big licorice ice cream cone. She said the most charming thing: "Everybody tells me I have such beautiful lavender eyes. A woman came up to me in Dior and said she just wanted to have a close look at my lavender eyes. They're not really lavender. If you ask me, when I get up in the morning and go to the bathroom and look in the bathroom mirror, they're gray. Just plain old gray."

I understand things haven't gone so well for her lately. If I were as beautiful as she is, I would think life would be filled with sweetness and light. I would hope my life would be a veritable festival of continuous adoration.

Most of my childhood I don't remember. It comes to me in flashes, and some things hang around, like the time I threw up on the floor in second grade, in public school, but most of it has faded, what it felt like, what it looked like, who was who. My sister, on the other hand, remembers everything.

The first year at May Day I was an oriole, for the dance of the birds—there was a cardinal and a robin and a blue jay and so on—which meant my mother had to sew an elaborate costume out of crepe paper involving a bird's head and a beak and wings with many feathers, all black and orange, a cross between Batman and Nijinsky, things you wouldn't normally make out of crepe paper and which you had to buy out of your own pocket as your contribution to the pageant, like bringing the pint of cream, heavy whipping cream, on Butter Day.

I loved my bird costume. I wish I still had it. It would cheer me up when I'm blue. Besides, the Orioles have always been my second favorite baseball team, and when I lived in Baltimore, going to Johns Hopkins, they were the best of the best.

My first-grade year in the May Day pageant, I was the crown bearer. This costume I still have a picture of. I was dressed in a huge white beret, probably sewn by my mother as well, and a white shirt with a white lace jabot and white shorts and white socks and black high-top sneakers. This costume was a mortification, even though I look happy in the picture. It's what you do, in pictures.

There was a May Pole, with streamers in eight different colors, all pinned to the ground, and eight different girls to pick them up and skip around the May Pole, twirling and untwirling the streamers, each wearing a dress that matched the color of her streamer, lavender and yellow and periwinkle blue and lime green and pink, all pale, the dresses all little coronation kind of things, all gauzy, all sewn by their mothers as well. In those days, mothers could do that kind of thing with their eyes closed.

And there were heralds and bumblebees and maids-in-waiting and pixies of all kinds, all in costumes sewn by their mothers, all the costumes identical every year. You could watch a decade of slides of the May Day pageant and every one of them would look the same.

There were masses of flowers everywhere, mostly lilacs and tulips. All the girls had little circlets of flowers in their hair. Like daisy chains. They had made them themselves the day before.

So there was a lot of cavorting and bird dancing and streamer twirling and bumblebee buzzing and heralding and bowing and scraping, all to a soundtrack of classical music played by Mrs. Lackman on her old record player on the porch, and then there was the coronation and then it was over. It took a lot of rehearsal. We had to rehearse inside when it was raining, but it was worth it. It always came off without a hitch. Even the schizophrenic son behaved on May Day.

The school shut its doors a long time ago and Mrs. Lackman is dead, but I wish I could see the May Day pageant just one more time before I die. I see myself in my splendid oriole costume, wings flapping, feathers fluttering in the breeze, or in a white lace jabot and high-tops, carrying a crown of flowers through billowing pastel streamers. But I could be wrong.

My memories are vague, as I said, and perhaps not accurate. Maybe "he look lak he a monf ole awready" was part of a Christmas pageant, which we probably also had one of. Maybe it was said about the Baby Jesus and not about George Washington. I don't know.

None of us who went to Mrs. Lackman's really remembers anything except the pageants, and the roles we played. We don't remember a thing about the actual school part. Except Butter Day, which was supposed to be vaguely educational.

I see my own childhood as though it happened to someone else, some person I don't recognize, just a series of brief moving pictures in which I am an insignificant figure.

Somewhere in the midst of all this pageantry came Butter Day, somewhere between Washington's Birthday and May Day. We didn't have to wear costumes, we didn't have to memorize anything, we just had to show up with a pint of cream.

We would sit in Mrs. Lackman's kitchen, the only time we were ever allowed in there, even when she would bake us cookies, which she did once in a blue moon. In fact, the only rooms we ever saw were the two classrooms, since apparently nobody was ever allowed to use the bathroom, and the kitchen was all sort of warm and homey compared to the classrooms, one of which had a high chair in the middle of it. Just in case.

Her son was away in the far reaches of the house, being loony, no doubt, but loony on his own time. We were safe. We were glad Butter Day had arrived.

We would sit in the kindergarten chairs, which had been taken into the kitchen and placed in a perfect circle. Mrs. Lackman would get out a group of Mason jars, blue-green glass with lids and screw-on tops, and fill each one half full with heavy cream.

Then we would take the Mason jars and distribute them. The children who got to go first would hold the jar as though it were the Holy Grail, the white cream bluish inside the jar. Then, at Mrs. Lackman's signal, the first children would begin to shake the jars. After a time, Mrs. Lackman would give another signal and the jars would be passed to the right, and the next child would begin to shake the jar, and so on around and around the circle.

The cream would froth in the jar and then begin to thicken like whipped cream. And then the miracle occurred.

The cream would begin to turn into butter. Liquid would separate from the bulk of the cream, and the clotted part would begin to turn a greenish yellow inside the jar.

We would keep shaking, shaking now like mad, since the object of our efforts was so close at hand. Mrs. Lackman was in a state of high excitement, and her exhortation would keep our arms, now tired from exertion, flailing away.

The cream was now round globs inside the jar, and made a kind of wet thunk as it went up and down, up and down, hitting the top and bottom of the jar, the useless, thin, milky liquid sloshing around the yellow mass.

Finally it was time to stop. Mrs. Lackman would open the jars, and inside each one there would be a round ball of butter. Soft, fresh butter.

Mrs. Lackman would put the butter on a chilled plate and get out a box of Saltine crackers and hand two crackers to each child. She would then take a butter knife and, going around the circle, spread a thin smear of butter on one of the two crackers, and each child, in a hysteria of excitement, would begin to eat the cracker in tiny, mouselike bites, except for the May King, who would put the whole thing in his enormous, athletic mouth and eat it in one bite.

When the first cracker was gone, Mrs. Lackman would move around the circle and, as though she were Lady Bountiful giving us far more than we deserved, spread an even thinner smear of butter on the second cracker.

We were pretty bored by that time, and our arms were tired, and some people were sweating from all the exertion of shaking the jar with great force, up and down, up and down. But we ate our crackers. The butter was delicious, unsalted, fresh, gleaming pale yellow. Two crackers of it was pretty much a surfeit, but with only one cracker, we would have felt a little cheated after all that effort.

Then Mrs. Lackman would smooth out each little glob of butter until it was a perfect soft ball and wrap it in wax paper and put it in her icebox and the true purpose of Butter Day was finally revealed. Mrs. Lackman wanted butter. Free butter. Free fresh butter. We had been given a minute taste of the delicacy Mrs. Lackman and her schizo son would enjoy for weeks.

Then we went back to learning to read and add, the first graders left totally to their own devices, the kindergartners harassed by her totally totalitarian method of learning and trying to go to the bathroom. Butter Day usually ended about when it was time for my red-headed neighbor to pee on the floor, although we'd gotten pretty used to it by then and it lacked the excitement it had originally held.

So that was Butter Day. Educational, fun, and, ultimately,

He Was So Fat

When we were little children, if my brother and sister and I wanted something really badly and all other entreaties had failed, there was one that always did the trick. We'd work ourselves up to an anguished howl and say, "But Mama, I need it. I need it for school." You had to sound really frustrated and kind of heartbroken, but it worked whether the desired item was a box of pencils or a new pair of roller skates. Needing something for school was unassailable, even though we never had any money.

I wanted this certain new pair of sneakers or a new plaid flannel shirt, something, anything that hadn't already been worn half to death by my brother, and even sometimes people before him; I wanted some new and wholly mine thing in the worst kind of way, but we had no money, and so I had to resort to the need-it-for-school argument, and that broke my mother down and she agreed. "Oh, all right," she said. She sent me to Mr. Swink's dry goods store in town, where I was told to charge it. "Put it on the never never," as my aunt used to say.

All the store owners knew us. There weren't any credit cards. You just signed for it. Years before, my mother used to stop in Mr. McCoy's grocery store after school and charge money so she servitude to Mrs. Lackman's private appetites. I can picture her, sitting down with her psychopathic son, slathering free butter on large steaming baked potatoes and wallowing in a swelter of gastronomic sensuality.

We got through it all. Except for the lack of opportunity to go to the bathroom, it was actually kind of fun, and public school, which we all started in the second grade, seemed drab in comparison. The teachers there were kind and smart, and were infinitely indulgent with the one-finger, two-finger system of education, which I gather was pretty general in those days. I've talked to other people.

The only exciting part of public school was atomic bomb drills, when we would either get under our desks, which was fun, or be herded into the dark and rat-infested boiler room, which was not fun, but which gave us a better, more bitter taste of life in an atomic holocaust.

Mrs. Lackman may have been a fascist dictator, and she may have abused the child labor laws, but we did learn to read. We learned to add and subtract. And we learned to sit for hours at a time at long tables with other attractive, well-mannered boys and girls and not make one single peep, except for the occasional, very occasional moments when Mrs. Lackman would stick her head in the door and ask how we were doing.

And, given a couple of pints of heavy cream — heavy whipping cream — and, of course, a Mason jar with a really tight-fitting lid and one of those rubber rings that goes inside it, I could still make a pound or two of butter, even if I were in the desert, even if I were in the frozen, barren tundra, even all by myself without one single hope of salvation, even without so much as a single Saltine cracker. You just shake the jar.

could go to the movies. She had an amazing amount of gall, my mother. And she always got away with it.

McCoy's sold McCormick spices and they had, in the window, a thermometer advertising the company. The different temperatures were marked by different spices, so one hundred degrees was chili pepper and so on down through whatever spices they could think of that corresponded in some metaphorical way to various temperatures. One cold day my grandmother ran into a friend of hers who said, "Yesterday it was lemon, but today it's all the way down to ginger!"

So I wanted these new sneakers or whatever it was, some trivial thing, and my mother finally relented because I needed it for school and all, and I decided, one Saturday afternoon in September, to walk to town and get them. It was two miles, and you walked down the creek, which was almost violently sexy—you could take your clothes off and nobody would see you or if somebody did see you maybe Something Big would happen; you saw old beer bottles and crumpled packs of cigarettes and used rubbers, and every single thing was invested with a kind of erotic promise. You could get rubbers out of machines in gas stations for a quarter, in the foul-smelling bathrooms, and I knew what they were because my brother's friends had told me.

Then you left the willowed water and walked up a hill and across a big long field by the two-lane road, past a pond that was frighteningly rumored to have no bottom at all, ever, so if you fell in, you would never be found, not if they dredged the pond forever. Then you walked over the crest of a hill and you could see it, the town, spread out before you like Oz, and you walked down through the university campus and then you were on the actual sidewalks.

Town was an exciting place compared to where we lived, largely because there were other people there. It was great, living in the country, it was a bucolic extravaganza, and it provided an almost endless number of ways to play, what with mud-clod wars and the endlessly cool waterfall in the creek and blacksnakes in the bedrooms and everything.

My brother and sister both had bicycles, but I never had one, even though, as one of my mother's friends recently remarked, every child in America had a bicycle. My mother said I could ride my brother's bike when he wasn't using it, but when do you use a bicycle except after school and on the weekends? At night? Alone at night? So I was often left to my own devices while they were off careening down gravel roads and hurtling into creeks where they sustained any number of life-threatening injuries involving trips to the emergency room.

One hot summer day I was in my grandmother's dining room and she had these gauzy curtains, her summer curtains, just fine light gauze, as fine and pretty as a bride's veil. They were blowing gently in the breeze and they were just irresistible, so I took out some matches and set them on fire. I just simply thought on a sweltering August day that it would be a fine thing to do. I actually did it twice, in both my grandmothers' houses, at different times. Then I crawled under the dining room table to watch the flames creep up the walls. I sat there watching my grandmothers' fluid curtains burn and waiting to be punished. It was both gut-wrenchingly magical and masochistic at the same time. Curtains like that are probably totally flame-retardant now.

So there was an almost endless number of hilarious things to do. But the almost endless part was very important, and there were many, many things that town had that we didn't have. Store windows. Ammonia Cokes. Movies. Rednecks with their sinewy forearms and hollowed-out chests lounging around by the Rockbridge National Bank, which was run by Mr. Rader, who knew everything about everybody, rednecks in their overalls spitting tobacco on Main Street. New clothes nobody else had worn. An alleyway you felt a little creepy walking through.

It was a nice day. Virginia in the fall is exactly the right temperature, the kind of temperature you imagine dreams would be in, if dreams had thermometers. It has both the nostalgia of summer's end, like a stove slowly cooling after you've turned it off, and the anticipation of almost everything else, the color, the cold, the clear hazeless air, the earth with a thin crust of sparkling frost, and, in the distance, the mountains a deep, true indigo.

It was a nice day and I was walking to town, where there were people and you could get lost in the crowd, although there wasn't really a crowd, and it would have been hard to get lost, since there were only six stoplights and most of the people knew who I was anyway. But I was walking to town and the new sneakers or the new shirt would somehow magically make my life more, well, more acceptable. I would be the envy of all. I would be good-looking and strong and dark and intense instead of just superficially clever. So, in a way, now that I think of it, I really did need this thing for school.

In the middle of the big field, I saw a group of boys I knew from school. They were in my grade and they were smoking cigarettes, just walking along with a vague air of bored menace.

And then they saw me, and they started my way. There was nowhere to go, the road was far off, and I knew them from school, and I never imagined that I was myself in any kind of trouble.

The leader of the gang was George Hazelwood. He was surrounded by five other boys—well, they weren't exactly boys; I mean, some of them shaved already, having failed various grades in their tortured academic careers, failed more than one. They all had hair like Elvis. Bad Elvis hair, lank and dirty and greasy. The oldest one, Henry MacLaine, was probably fifteen. Henry MacLaine was really, really stupid. He was fifteen and he was only in the eighth grade. You have to be pretty stupid for that.

George Hazelwood was the leader of the gang because he was so fat. He was rotund. Rednecks tend to be either fat or really, really skinny. George was the kind of white trash fat you get from eating too many sandwiches made out of Merita bread and peel-off baloney and biscuits fried in lard and everything else boiled in fatback, which is a kind of glutinous form of salt.

We were all, my sister and brother and I, preternaturally skinny, because we never ate any kind of snack food that came out of a bag and we never ate between meals and we never had Cokes, unless we went to visit the Learys, where they had potato chips and Fritos and dip, something we weren't even allowed to say, much less to eat except when we were there (or at the Fords', who also had dip). The Learys always kept a case of Cokes on the back porch from the bottling plant on Route 60. When you took a Coke, you put a nickel in the little hole in the crate, and when all the Cokes were gone, the nickels paid for a new case.

The whole conglomeration of boys, fat and skinny, surrounded me, giving me the kind of grunts that pass for *hello* in that set, and they asked what y'all doing and I said I was walking to town, and then they all pulled in a little closer.

"You ain't sorry?" Henry MacLaine asked me.

"Sorry for what?"

"Sorry for that thing you said to George last Saturday in town, right in front of the Rockbridge National Bank."

"I never saw George last Saturday. I don't even think I was in town."

"Yes you was. Wasn't he George?"

"Yep. He was definitely in town."

It kind of took me aback that George Hazelwood could use the word *definitely* in a sentence.

"And you said some things. You said something to George in front of the Rockbridge National Bank. Right smack in front of the bank."

"I—"

"You said, 'George Hazelwood, suck my dick.'"

"I did not." I didn't even know what it meant to suck somebody's dick. I don't think I had ever heard the word *dick* before, but even I could figure out that, whatever it meant, it wasn't something you said to a fat, greasy, lard-soaked classmate in front of the bank.

"That's right. You said, 'George Hazelwood, you suck my dick.'"

They were stupid, they were socially and economically dispossessed, and they didn't know I was wearing my brother's old clothes. They thought I was one of Them, the ones they did yard work for, the ones whose silver their mothers cleaned, the ones whose driveways their drunken fathers plowed when it snowed or whose garbage they carried to the dump.

Then George Hazelwood pulled something out of his pocket. "You see this?" he said. "This here is a switchblade. My brother brought it back from the army. It's got a real long blade on it." And then he pushed a button, and the blade flashed out and it was, in fact, really long and it looked really sharp, and I was surrounded by a group of my actual classmates who had pulled a knife on me in the middle of a perfect Saturday afternoon on which I was going to acquire the one thing that was going to make all the difference, just by signing my mother's name in Mr. Swink's book.

I was very short at the time. The autumn grass was up over my waist. I weighed ninety pounds. George Hazelwood wasn't much taller, and he never would be, but he was so fat and he had a switchblade in his hand.

George Hazelwood was quivering with venom. He was like an enormously fat, dirty-nailed, acned, pig-eyed redneck pudding, and the thing that was clear and steady in my eye was the faces of the boys around me, and the very long, very sharp blade that was getting closer to my face. I could tell that these boys really didn't admire me very much. You could tell they didn't think a new flannel shirt or a sharp pair of Keds would make much difference in my general persona.

"We don't like that. We don't like that kind of talk, do we, George?" Henry was not about to let go of this.

"I don't suck dick," said George, and he said it in such a way that I knew, whatever sucking dick was, it was just not in George's best interest to do it. Not at all. "That wasn't very nice."

"I didn't say it."

"Yes you did. Nobody says shit like that to me."

He was kind of like this guy who moved to town later in my life, when I was a teenager. He called himself the Wild Man of Chicago, so I guess he had lived there, and he wanted in the worst way to kill a local real estate broker who had crossed him in some vague way. There was no apparent reason for this, nobody knew what the source of the dispute was, or how long ago it had taken place, but there was also no reason to believe that the Wild Man wasn't serious when he said it.

"And you know how I'm going to do it?" said the Wild Man. "I'm going to sneak into his house one night, when he's in the shower before going to bed, and I'm going to stab him in the heart while he's standing there. And you want to know why? Because that is the most humiliating way for a man to die. Nekkid."

George Hazelwood was kind of like a juvenile version of the Wild Man. "You see this knife?" he said. And I really, really did. I really did see the knife in George Hazelwood's hand.

"You just might get to town missing one of your ears. I just maybe might have to cut one of your ears off."

That's when I said the stupid thing. It was one of the most stupid things I have ever said, and the humiliation of it haunts me still.

I said, "George, I seriously doubt it." My tone was so acerbic, so dripping with hauteur and acid, you would have thought I was one of the characters in a Noël Coward play. You would have thought I was Lew Ayres playing the drunken brother in *Holiday*, by Philip Barry. I was twelve years old. I was four-foot-eleven and I chose that exact moment to behave like an asshole toward a fat juvenile delinquent with a switchblade in his hand.

The minute I said it, I knew it was the wrong thing to say. It was worse than saying "Suck my dick," because at least only tough guys said something like that, whereas etiolated wimps said, "I seriously doubt it."

The switchblade moved up until it was just under the lobe of my ear. I could feel how sharp it was. George Hazelwood's hand was steady as a rock and the other boys' eyes gleamed with bloodlust and impatience. George was standing so close to me I could smell the wood smoke in his pathetically worn shirt.

Then we heard it. We heard singing. We heard a group of girls singing "Over hill, over dale," and then a flag appeared on the crest of the hill behind us, blowing and snapping in the breeze, and it was carried by Kathleen McKenna, who marched resolutely over the hill in full Girl Scout regalia, leading a troop of other Girl Scouts who marched double file singing, "Over hill, over dale," Girl Scouts who wore not only their full uniforms, berets and everything, but also sashes with all their medals for making slipknots and starting fires with two sticks of wood and whatnot. They were so young and healthy and white.

Kathleen saw me and waved, although she did not veer from her chosen course. In fact, all the girls waved in their Hitler youth fervor, and when I looked up again, George Hazelwood and his troop of boys had vanished. They just weren't there anymore and my ear was still on my head. I had been improbably saved from mutilation by the Girl Scouts of America.

I calmly walked on to town and bought the whatever it was. I did get nervous about walking home, though, and I called my mother and she said, "Oh, all right," and she came and got me from Mr. Swink's. I never told anybody why I had decided not to walk back from town, right in the middle of naptime.

When I saw George and Henry and the gang at school, they averted their eyes; in fact, they averted their eyes until the actual days when they all, one by one, dropped out of school.

The thing I bought made absolutely no difference at all, and I have spent my whole life looking over hill, over dale for one thing and another, the one thing that would make the difference between who I was and who I wanted to be. An Italian suit or a cashmere sweater, bought from a saleswoman at Bergdorf's who knows me by name. She even called me after 9/11 to see if I was intact. A fancy car. A lovely house with an orchard on the beach in a country where I did not speak the language. Having my underwear ironed by a woman from Granada. Christmas. A touch on the cheek from some loving hand, some kiss on the mouth, some tangled embrace in the dark, however awkward; one obsession after another, knowing everything would fail, like the sneakers or the flannel shirt, knowing nothing would last, but something, something that would tell me that, finally, I was not helpless, I was not small, I was not weak or ugly or poor, that I didn't have some fat redneck holding a knife to my ear on a beautiful day when I could see the mountains indigo blue beyond the sharp edge of the switchblade.

Some something that would mitigate the terrible beauty and unassuageable sadness of life.

I have never found it. I will look forever.

How I Went On

Here's my question: How did they go on? Knowing what they knew, and knowing that each knew the thing the other knew, although my grandmother, I suppose, was alone in what she knew; I mean, I guess she never told anybody. I know she never told anybody, never discussed what she probably couldn't hold in her mind after I had told her what had happened, after what I told her, even if I understood what had happened myself. I mean, nobody knew, because years after, after I had been in the hospital, in the bin, my aunt said to me she thought I'd had a breakdown because I was sad about my mother's breast cancer and I just thought, Jesus. I mean, you don't have a psychotic break and slit your wrists because your mother has only one breast. My grandmother went on with her daughter's wedding and her husband's dying, went on baking bread and making a breakfast for herself, every morning, and carrying it on a lap tray up to her bedroom so she could have breakfast in bed, couldn't deal with what had happened only the night before, because it was so far outside the realm of what her life, even her life as a nurse, as the wife of a doctor, had taught her was possible. How did they go on? Any of them? All of them?

How did they go on doing the things that people do, getting up in the morning, getting dressed, making coffee in a mottled old tin percolator on the stove, waiting for the brown liquid to bubble up in the little glass bell, waiting for hope or for the next party, serving breakfast for a family of five, going off to work in cars on which the windshields were frozen over with frost so that the morning glare glittered and blinded you when you turned out of the driveway onto the highway, into the east, teaching young cadets the brazen march of British history, bathing, putting on girdles, putting on lipstick, putting curlers in their hair, giving my grandmother a perm every month or so, playing bridge on Wednesdays—every Wednesday—with limeade and cucumber sandwiches with the edges cut off and paprika sprinkled on top for color, reading, reading the *New Yorker,* reading the novels of John Updike and John Cheever and Walker Percy and writing reviews of these novels for the *Roanoke Times,* reviews that were witty and astute, discussing these novels with their professor friends and their wives, the wives who in those days didn't do anything except raise children and keep up so they could be smart and witty at cocktail parties, discussing these books in the winter when snow was falling and I had made popcorn for the grownups because it was a cheap hors d'oeuvres and there was a fire in the fireplace?

How did they go on ironing clothes and polishing the silver and teaching us to make snow angels and snow ice cream and real burnt sugar and almond ice cream from my grandmother's famous recipe in a hand-cranked freezer in the summer, buying shaved ice in big brown paper bags from the ice house, leaving their socks on the floor and their suits thrown on chairs for my

mother to pick up—that's how spoiled he was—and sending
off to Thalheimer's in Richmond for tweed Davidow suits, one
a year because they were so expensive? How did they go on making ends meet, giving us birthday parties, making marvelous
cakes shaped like lambs and covered with coconut for Easter,
buying cows by the quarter and keeping them butchered in the
freezer in the cabin where there was also a real icebox, the old-
fashioned kind you used to keep cool with ice, helping children
with their homework, helping us with the intricacies of algebra,
watching as we made grades that would make any parent proud,
my brother and me, watching my sister struggle in school because she had a teacher in sixth grade who told her she would
never be as smart as her brothers, trying to help her through the
trauma, trying to get her to study and stop coloring her hair, she
was so beautiful, and giving her riding lessons, and sending my
brother and sister off to dancing school, my sister in white
gloves, where they learned to waltz and fox-trot and do the box
step, but not me, leaving me out of it, leaving me to watch as my
friends went to dancing school and I didn't, when all the nice
children in town went to dancing school in suits and ties and
crinolines and white gloves when they were twelve, reading the
novels of Salinger and endless cheap mysteries, going to dances
where they wore white dinner jackets and dresses down to the
floor, learning to cook French food in cooking classes once a
week, letting me start sending my shirts to the laundry when I
was thirteen because I was old enough, lying in bed and hearing me in my bed tell stories to the whole family, an endless
story of my real parents, Solly and Blanche —Jewish—who had
carelessly lost me one day, left me behind in their travels, Solly

and Blanche who were truck drivers and carried cabbages from
coast to coast and left me in the back one day with the vegetables and hit a bump in the road so I bounced out of the truck just
as my parents were driving by and so my parents had adopted
me (my parents weren't my real parents), trying to write novels
and poems themselves and coming up short, mixing cocktails
and giving and going to endless parties, sending my brother off
to a fancy prep school on his godfather's money, letting a family
friend, who remembered being in the womb, or so he said, who
could recite *Paradise Lost* in its entirety, or so he said, buy me my
first suit, a heavy gray wool tiny suit, so I could go off to the
Cuban Embassy in Washington and receive a medal they had
awarded to my grandfather because he had done a remarkably
brave thing and helped find the cure for yellow fever in Cuba
with Walter Reed but my grandfather had died and my grandmother was too bereft to go herself, and I was named after him,
so I went in a sweltering wool suit on a hot Washington day,
than which there is no hotter, me a little boy of six among all
these sweet old people who were also getting medals, who didn't
look so very brave or valorous anymore, just kind and happy and
old, and the Cuban ambassador kissed me on my cheek and my
picture was in the paper it was so cute, and making crab salad
to put in hollowed out tomatoes for a summer supper, letting
each child have one thing he wouldn't eat because one day my
brother said if he ate sweet potatoes he would throw up and my
mother made him and he threw up all over the table? How did
they go on?

How did they go on buying us new shoes in the store where
they had a machine where you stood on a step in your new shoes

and stuck your feet inside and looked through a little window to see an X-ray of your toes inside the shoes to see if they fit, so probably we're all going to get cancer from all those rays, but it was fun anyway, we didn't know, or putting on earrings or tying a necktie, or going to see my grandmother, my father's mother, who didn't think my mother was good enough, and my mother hated going there, hated every minute of it, and going to the beach for two weeks every summer until my father inherited $100,000 in 1964 and after that we had Mustang convertibles and went to the beach for three weeks, and my mother loved the beach and went in the water once a year in bathing suits that were beautiful and fit her beautifully, bathing suits of white pique with strawberries embroidered on them, bathing suits with little skirts, and we'd take everything to the beach, all our groceries because everything at the beach was too expensive, and beach chairs and coolers and bed linens so we looked like the Joads, and reading Josephine Tey mysteries and passing them on to us, the story of the sick detective who decides to solve the mystery of Richard III and the little princes in the tower, and reading John Fowles and Tom Wolfe, who came from Rich-mond, who once appeared in Richmond in khakis and a plain blue shirt and said he was traveling incognito, whose first book I reviewed for the *Roanoke Times,* at the age of thirteen, how did they continue?

How did they go on gardening, my father putting in an elab-orate garden every year and then mostly abandoning it, or at least abandoning the parts that required too much labor, my mother putting in a beautiful rose garden and being proud of it and then uprooting all the roses and moving them farther from

the house, for the sun, she said, and then farther and farther, until finally it was just too far to walk and she didn't take care of
them anymore and they all died, rust and beetles and black spot
and mildew, neglect, and making me go back into the store and
return a pack of Life Savers I'd stolen from the A&P where they
had live lobsters in tanks and I walked into the store in dead
mortification, but Bertha Townes saw me and gave me a nickel
to pay for the candy, and living through the illnesses, the mumps
and strep throat, which had killed my aunt Sally Page, and
measles and whooping cough and the cuts and scrapes and broken bones that children get by the dozens, and my sister getting
a pussy willow bud so buried in her ear and getting so hysteri-
cal about it that she had to go to the hospital and be put under
a general anesthetic before they could get it out, and the dead
dogs, darling Frederick the dachsund and Bruce Catton the bea-
gle and James Bond and Moll Flanders the basset hounds, and
Leamus the cat, who wandered in from the cold, like the spy,
and the oyster stew a few days before Christmas and the big dinner on Christmas Eve and writing a letter to Santa, which we
burned in the fireplace, watching the ashes go up the chimney
and fly on through the cold night sky to the North Pole, and
listening, every Christmas Eve, to an old record of Charles
Laughton reading *Mr. Pickwick's Christmas* until we all knew it
by heart, and making us line up on the steps on Christmas
morning in the order of our ages, until my father had gotten the
fire going in the fireplace and my mother had made her first cup
of coffee, the percolator all ready from the night before, and
serving us Thanksgiving dinner on Wednesday night because
my mother hated Thanksgiving, she thought somebody would

force her to eat dinner at some odd hour, so we had nothing to
do all day Thanksgiving, except listen to VMI play VPI on the
radio, and the endless laundry and the endless ironing and
the conversation and the fights, and having a big party on the
Fourth of July, with fireworks brought all the way from the Key-
stone Fireworks Corporation in Pennsylvania that you shot out
of a four-inch mortar in the back yard dense with trees and nobody cared, and nobody thought of the danger and everybody
left the minute the fireworks were over because it was dark and
the children were overstimulated, the smoke hanging thick and
acrid in a cloud over the back yard, like a battlefield in World
War I, and making love in the bed in which it happened, in
which it began, the bed I threw out last year, they must have,
they were obsessed with each other, they thought they were the
couple everybody wanted to be, and listening to me weeping and
telling the story of how the McClouds threw me out of their
house in a blizzard at nine o'clock at night because they were
drunk and crazy, saying who did I think I was and how my
family thought we were better than anybody else, which we
did, actually, but it went on for hours while they served me
SpaghettiOs out of the cold can and powdered milk they hadn't
even bothered to stir up while their children sat silent and mortified across the room and finally they threw me out even though
it was snowing so hard you could barely see your hand in front
of your face, all because I was an hour late to come over and
spend the night because there was a blizzard and I had to wait
until the cocktail party broke up and Pax and Sis drove me in
because my father wasn't going to put down his drink and get
in a car in that weather if he didn't have to and I should have

called but I didn't, or maybe I did and they forgot because the McClouds were so drunk, and when they threw me out I struggled up a hill to get to my aunt's, my little overnight bag in my hand, but I kept crying and falling and I was twelve and when I got to my aunt's house she thought I'd been in a car accident because I was crying too hard to tell her what really happened so she felt all my bones to see if anything was broken, and Skip had to bring his Jeep and drive me home and my grandmother listened to the whole story and said, "Well, you lie down with the dogs, you get up with the fleas"; how did they go on changing the sheets when you were sick, making you change your pajamas and move into their bed while she put fresh, clean sheets on your bed and waited for your fever to go down, her hand so cool on your hot forehead, on your hair, how did they do it?

How did they go on laughing at jokes they heard, laughing at cartoons in the *New Yorker* where the people, even the Cheever people, led the lives they imagined for themselves, lives of sophistication and adultery and bitterness and cocktails and irony, sermons and soda water, and, yes, reading John O'Hara, and making Christmas presents for friends because they didn't have all that much money, and making applejack out of cider we squeezed on a day when my brother had a hangover so he almost threw up, and making clever carving boards and bread boards and entertaining the Episcopal cadets with big pots of spaghetti and garlic bread and having my grandmother's friend Nell Baker come for a month in August from the house where she lived in the Plains, and telling people he had caddied once for Gloria Swanson at the Fredericksburg Country Club although it wasn't true, and going to my father's mother's house and sitting in the stifling heat and eating those big meals in the middle of the day, and telling endless stories about things that had happened decades before, stories they told over and over the way you do, each new audience a fresh chance, trying to make contact, trying to make an impression of insouciance and glamour, Gloria Swanson and all, and about how my father bought a Turner watercolor for ten dollars in New York when he was a little boy when he went there on a trip with his father and it really is, it really is a Turner watercolor, and I've seen a picture of him and his father with the Empire State building behind them, and my mother telling everybody about how, on their honeymoon in New York, my father had undertipped and the waiter had followed them out of the restaurant and spit in my father's face, and spanking their children with a hairbrush or a belt when we were bad, although not very hard, and having drinks with Edward Albee and meeting Arnold Toynbee and Muriel Rukeyser, and Carson McCullers and Katherine Anne Porter, and reading John le Carré and James Thurber and Michael Arlen—*Exiles,* my mother's favorite book that year, it was always on her bedside table, she must have read it half a dozen times, she knew the whole story before she turned the first page—and wearing red tartan silk dresses with white lace inserts for a fancy dinner for the Barretts when the table was set with red glasses and all the gleaming silver and the best china, and cleaning all the Canton in the corner cupboard once a year, my grandmother saying the reason there weren't any dinner plates was that my mother had broken them all as a child, one plate for every tantrum, and my father calling me when I was fourteen into the sitting room where they were having drinks with two other couples so I could show everybody my Adam's apple and they all laughed, and, in the summer, putting slipcovers made of white linen and red piping on all the furniture, slipcovers that Lula Hall had made, and choosing new materials—we never said fabrics—to recover old family furniture, blue velvets and cheap brocades and tapestries, and buying cheap new furniture from Schewel's, so that somebody once said there wasn't a single comfortable place to sit in our whole sitting room except the chair my mother always sat in, and making sweet bread and butter pickles in the summer and bitter marmalade in the winter, sterilizing the bottles, sealing the marmalade with melted paraffin, and being just regular people, just ordinary people of their time and class, until my grandmother got old and her friends got old so they wouldn't make the trip out to the country and come down our treacherous sidewalk to play bridge on Wednesdays when the weather was bad, leaving her with all those sandwiches, and my parents began to fall apart by degrees so fewer people came for drinks and they went out less often and the colleges didn't have fancy dances anymore so the fancy dresses rotted to ruin in the closet, and my mother had a cleaning woman, Bertis Dean, who came and kept everything in some semblance of order and a man Alexander Smothers to come once a week in a stinking truck to take the garbage—he got paid two dollars and a shot of whiskey—but she went on making dinners and welcoming us home from school with our favorites and they tried, they really did, to be good parents, and discussing books with us, and sitting by the radiator in the winter and reading mystery stories and poetry by Ngaio Marsh and Robert Bly, how did they go on?

What did they remember? How much did they forget?

How did they go on learning crewelwork and making their own clothes and him writing a column for a finky little Virginia magazine, columns that people loved for their facile charm and wrote letters about after he died, and writing for *American Heritage* and *Holiday* and once for the *New Yorker*, a funny story about my father's cousin breaking a rib while he was out duck hunting and he rolled under a barbwire fence, a bob wire fence as we called it, and rolled over a box of Marlboro cigarettes and heard his bone crack, he was not without distinction or talent, my father, and falling into blind rages at each other, except my grandmother who lived to be ninety-four, knowing what she knew, or forgetting what she had never really heard about what happened, and whom I never saw angry except that snowy day when her friends wouldn't come to play bridge, and my mother and father coming to my graduation and eating crab salad in my apartment in Baltimore with my roommate and his parents and then listening while I gave a speech to the whole graduation assembly in which I described the relentless viciousness and occasional grace of university life in the late sixties, so critical of my college that the president wouldn't shake my hand when he gave me my diploma, but some members of the faculty stood and applauded and a man came up to me at dinner at Hausner's that night, a restaurant that was famous for having the biggest ball of string in the world, came up with tears in his eyes and told me how moved he'd been, and I competed in piano competitions, which I never won, and edited the school newspaper in high school, my mother writing thank-you notes famous for their warmth and politesse and perfection, going to the Homestead to ride in sleighs through the winter snows, and going to house parties, going to the movies to see *South Pacific,* and asking the children to set the table, to do their homework, to mind their manners, to write thank-you notes on Christmas afternoon while they took their naps, and reading in bed, and smoking Larks, so that we could hear the strike of the match after the alarm went off on school days, my mother smoking in the morning dark in bed, before she put her feet on the floor, just like I do now, and going to bed, my father in his boxer shorts, my mother in her thin nightgowns, and being the kind of people they were, bright and generous and eager for the next thing, and then less and less so, until finally they would start the pickles and let them rot in the crock, until finally she didn't make apple butter anymore and my grandmother got too old to make marmalade so she bought it off the shelf, Dundee, in little white pottery jars, and then she died in her peaceful way, and my mother and father went on until they didn't care enough to read or dress or cut their own toenails or defend themselves against alcoholism and cancer and filthiness and disrepair and rats in the house, how did they go on?

I know how I went on, but here is my question: How did they live a life, knowing what they knew, how did they thrive for so long and then fail? How did they go on?

The Cowboy Sandwich

Before we got the cowboy outfits, we got the Roman outfits. There was a gold plastic breastplate, with strong pecs with raised nipples and awesome abs, and there was a centurion's helmet and a plastic sword. It was purely an upper body thing, we didn't get little skirts or anything, or gold shin guards, so we had to put on all this gear with our blue jeans and sneakers. It was not exactly a Steve Reeves look, but my brother and I were pretty impressed. After Christmas had gone, however, we found that the Roman centurion outfits lacked a certain something. They lacked staying power. They lacked pith.

Perhaps it was the wide, unbridgeably wide disparity between our own boys' bodies and the men's bodies meant to fit snugly inside the breastplate. Perhaps there was something about the straps, or the dinky plastic sword, or our own total lack of knowledge about the Roman Empire, but there was something missing, and the outfits were soon relegated to the miasma of the toy chest.

But when we were six and eight, my older brother and I got matching cowboy outfits for Christmas. There was a vest in a kind of pinto pattern, with a sheriff's badge, a checked flannel shirt, and a wide-brimmed cowboy hat, which was black. There was a belt with holsters and a pair of six-shooters.

My God, we loved those costumes. We had a large place in the country and we could find infinite ways of playing good guys and bad guys and badlanders and, well, cowboys. Cowboys we knew something about.

We had actually been to a 3-D cowboy movie that showed Indians throwing sharp spears straight at your face so you had to duck to avoid them. A man almost died of thirst before finding a pond of brackish water. We went to bunches of cowboy movies, regular 2-D ones. People had gunfights and they wore fringed buckskins and bolo ties and they fell in love with school-teachers and there was always Katy Jurado and all kinds of things happened to fire your imagination and we remembered all of it.

I have a photograph that shows the two of us in our cowboy clothes. Our hats are tilted back on our heads. We look proud. We look happy.

The cowboy thing could have gone on forever, but something happened. It was so strange that it almost defies description, but it happened to us while we were still cowboys, just back from riding the range.

It was a cold day. We didn't care. It was such a change from going exploring or throwing mud clods at each other, which was how we usually passed our spare time, trying to come as close to a real injury as possible without actually having to go to the emergency room, so we were out riding the range, hunting down bad guys and blowing the thin trails of smoke away from our hot cap pistols, when our mother called us into lunch.

We didn't walk in. We sidled in. We had seen in the movies the way the cowboys would stalk into the saloons, walking actu-ally sort of the way runway models walk now, slinking, waiting for the first fire of the first tossed shot of bad whiskey, and we wanted to be everything they were and do everything they did.

We sat down at the yellow linoleum table in our tiny kitchen, and my mother served our lunch. Tuna fish sandwiches and a glass of milk. Grub.

We were total cowboys, except for the cheesy high-tops we had to wear because we didn't have cowboy boots, but that didn't matter when you had the swagger, the Western ethos in your bloodstream. We spoke in terse sentences. We said things like "pardner" and "pardon me, ma'am," although that wasn't so unusual since we addressed our mother as ma'am anyway.

I took off my hat so it lay against my back, held on by the chinstrap, and I began to eat. My brother, who was as dead stubborn as a box of nails, kept his hat flat on his head, his arms folded, but tense, ready, as though he might reach for his six-shooter at any moment and start shooting shot glasses off the shelf behind the bar.

"Eat your lunch, darling," said my mother.

"No ma'am," said my brother.

"You must be hungry. Your brother's eating his lunch."

"I could eat a horse, I'm so hungry."

"Then eat your lunch."

"Can't do it, ma'am."

"Why not?"

My brother turned a sardonic face toward her.

"I won't eat my lunch until you say, 'Eat your lunch, cowboy.'"

"What?"

"Eat your lunch, cowboy. Say it."

"You're being ridiculous. Eat your lunch."

My mother busied herself around the kitchen, getting things ready for supper or something. Five minutes passed. My brother stared ahead in stony silence.

My mother turned from the sink. She was getting irritated now.

"I thought I told you to eat your lunch."

"Not until you say, 'Eat your lunch, cowboy.'"

"I won't. I won't say it. And you will eat your lunch like your brother. Look. He's almost finished."

"Not until you say it."

I could feel real trouble brewing. For some reason, for some reason known only to housewives in the fifties, when tranquilizers were just beginning to be prescribed for the incredible boredom and desperation they felt, my mother just snapped. She just freaked the hell out. She refused to say it. She refused, and my brother, who was not on Miltowns, refused to eat.

"I told you to eat your lunch, and you're going to eat it."

"Nope."

Trouble was not only brewing, it was bubbling over. I finished my sandwich. I carried my plate and my glass to the sink. My brother had not moved a muscle. My mother sat down at the table across from him and they just stared at each other. If his six-shooter had had real bullets, he would have shot her. If her tranquilizers hadn't already kicked in, she would have strangled him. It was that intense.

I stood awkwardly in the kitchen, not knowing what to do, not knowing what was going to happen.

Nothing happened. Nothing happened for hours. The bread dried out around the edges. For awhile she tried to discuss it

with him. Then she realized that was futile and she just sat staring at him as his lunch grew stale. She shouted at him. She
pleaded. She threatened. Nothing.

He was more obstinate by the minute. So was she, despite the
Miltowns.

They had a hard lot, those mothers in the fifties. They were
home all day. They had to put bobby pins in their hair, pulling
them open with their teeth. Everything had to be perfect all the
time. And they had these children who had strange notions
picked up at the movies. They had children with perfect manners who were completely recalcitrant.

I wish I could remember how it all turned out. I wish I could
remember if he had to eat the tuna fish sandwich for dinner, or
whether he went to bed without any supper at all.

It must have ended. Life went on, after all. We grew up. I
don't remember whether we ever played at being cowboys again,
but we must have. It couldn't have been that big a deal.

My brother was stubborn, and he had a temper a mile wide.
He wasn't mean; he just got mad. He once threw a pencil at me
across the dining room, the pencil coming at my face like the
spear in the 3-D movie, and it stuck in my forehead like an ar-
row and drew real blood that trickled down into my eyes. I
walked into the middle of a cocktail party like a dork to show off
what he had done. The pencil was still in my forehead. What an
idiot. Now that was mean. I still have a tiny blue mark, just under the hairline.

Eat your lunch, cowboy. That's all she had to say. And she
wouldn't say it. Not that afternoon. Clearly not ever.

But on that day, there must have been some resolution. It must have ended by three o'clock, which was when my mother took her nap. We must have had supper. She had been fixing supper, and sitting down to it was a holy ritual: seven-thirty, everybody in place, everything lovely. Candles and silverware. My mother had a habit of making a delicious, complicated dinner in the morning when she was especially bored and all jacked up on coffee, not the meat part but things like creamed onions, and leaving it sitting on the stove all day, so sometimes it got a little frightening, but in general we sat down hungry and got up satisfied. Nobody ever had to be rushed to the hospital to have his stomach pumped.

Eat your lunch, cowboy. Four words. Life must have gone on. My mother adored my brother, everything he did made her love him even more, or laugh until she cried—he was that charming, and that smart, despite his temper.

But I know them both well enough to know that she never said it and he never ate the sandwich. That much is crystal clear.

Years later, my brother got kicked out of college. It was an unthinkable event. It was something nobody could comprehend. It was one of those things my parents wouldn't discuss with even their closest friends, as though my brother could somehow charm and cajole his way back into Williams and everything would be fine.

It was 1968, the war in Vietnam was raging, and the summer was filled with tears and acrimony and dread. Nobody could believe that my brilliant brother had not gone to class for six months. Nobody could believe that he had not turned in a single paper. Nobody could believe that he spent the entire time sleeping in his dorm room and going to parties, where he would be charming and drink beer all night. All his roommates were hard partygoers, but they also went to class and got fantastic grades, and they, too, were stunned and mystified by my brother's behavior. He had done brilliantly in prep school, he had read *War and Peace* when he was thirteen, and things like that just didn't happen in our family. Failure was less final, more mortal perhaps, but less irrevocable. It took a long time, failure, not like having somebody slam a door in your face and then turn the lock.

I have a clear picture of him, that winter before he flunked out. It is Winter Carnival; he is standing in a fisherman's knit sweater, facing away from me, his hair long, his shoulders hunched against the cold. He hadn't opened a letter in six months. He would stay in his room for days, just lie on his bed except to eat and collect anecdotes.

He was a social animal, that weekend, except that he went to bed early while I stayed up late talking to his roommates. You would never have known anything was wrong.

Spring Weekend, his roommates, Daddy Jim, who had a brother called Lunch Madrid, and Bart and Robin, told me while he was sleeping that he was going to flunk out, and I was so horrified I never told anybody, so that, when it happened, my parents somehow blamed me, because I knew and should have said something, as though they hadn't been getting his grades in the mail for a year. Maybe they just assumed. Maybe they didn't look at them, assuming.

Every day, every night of that hot summer, there were long discussions about what was to be done and what had happened and how it had happened. We went over it a thousand thousand times. And then we went out to parties to drink Pabst Blue Ribbon.

I had suggested that he needed to see a psychiatrist, but my mother said we didn't do things like that, we didn't air our private affairs in public, even if public meant the confidentiality of a shrink's office.

My mother was crying. She cried a lot that summer, a hopeless kind of drizzle that fell from her eyes almost all the time. She and my brother were Discussing the Situation.

"Just tell me," she pleaded, because my brother had remained mute about the whole thing, had not bothered to explain or justify his behavior in any way, just thrown around idle threats about becoming a conscientious objector or going to Canada like Jesse Winchester had done, "just tell me how all this began."

"I'll tell you exactly," said my brother. "It started because you wouldn't say, 'Eat your lunch, cowboy.'"

She stared at him for a long moment, as though he were still eight and standing in his chaps and his vest and his sheriff's badge and his six-shooters and his hat.

And then they both began to laugh hysterically. They laughed so hard they cried. They laughed until the sweltering afternoon turned cool and Lyndon Johnson was a cardboard cutout and every eye was blue and my brother's academic career was relentlessly brilliant and everybody was unremittingly kind. And that was the way we dealt with trauma and pain and sadness in my family. At least, that's the way we dealt with my brother.

Such Charming Hands

On the night of September 6, 1952, I woke up in the moonlit dark of a dead hot night to find that my father was fucking me. It was a month and two days after my fourth birthday.

I was a handsome little boy, beautiful my mother said. I didn't look a thing like I look now. I looked hopeful. I looked as though life was riveting with possibility.

I was in my mother and father's bed, in a pair of short striped pajamas. I was in my mother and father's bed because the next day was my aunt's wedding, and there were houseguests. I had gone to bed in my own bed and, after all the guests had left and the bartender Tiny had cleaned off the bar and washed all the glasses and the drinking had finally stopped for the night, I had been carried into my mother and father's bed so that one of the houseguests could sleep in mine. My mother and father were always having houseguests, house parties, and it wasn't a big house, it had five bedrooms but everybody was young and they liked camping out, and my parents were such lovely hosts, so the children were sort of shuffled around: my parents' bed, a chaise longue in my parents' room, or army cots set up in corners. Canvas and sticks in corners while the grownups snored in their underwear.

Two rooms away, my grandfather lay dying. He was wearing striped pajamas, too. His glasses were on the night table next to the bed. I had sat on his lap while he read to me. He was too sick to read now, but he had been kind and good-hearted and distant but good with children.

It was in one of these army cots I had the first dream I can remember. I don't remember how old I was, but it was before, it was just before the September night. I must have been three. It was during one of the house parties. I was on a cot in the corner. It was almost dawn.

I was in a big city, even though I had never been in a city, standing on the top of a tall skyscraper, even though I had never seen a skyscraper. There were three identical buildings, square and tall, arranged around a central space, with one side open to the city, the way Lincoln Center is today. Two of the buildings were navy blue aluminum and one, the one I was standing on the top of, was maroon.

As I peered down from the great height, as I was looking over the edge at the large square below, the wind blew and I fell off. I was a tiny child. I began to fall faster and faster, the ground rushing at me with terrifying speed. I could see the paving stones. As I got nearer to the ground, I began to slow in my descent, slowing and slowing until I was wafting downward, back and forth like an autumn leaf. When I was about three feet off the ground, a beautiful angel, a rococo angel out of the Bible story books, swooped down and grabbed me in his arms and held me gently like a pietà and flew up and into the sky and through the bright blue until he flew into my own room in the first light and deposited me gently in the cot in which I was sleeping.

I woke up and I was in the bed where I had started. There were grownups snoring softly in the room. The room smelled like liquor and night sweat. It was getting light out. The birds were beginning to sing.

Later, I used to dream that I was in a plane crash, before I had ever been in an airplane. The plane crashed into a tall building in a city. Everybody on the plane was killed, in the dream, but I walked away without a scratch. This happened over and over again, but the angel only caught me once.

When my grandfather died, two months after my aunt's wedding day, he was still wearing striped pajamas when they carried him, dead on a stretcher, not covered up or anything, just dead, down the stairs and up the walk. I remember how still he looked, how white. He didn't have his glasses on. I still have the tortoise-shell glasses he wasn't wearing.

Actually, at the moment I woke up, my father wasn't fucking me yet.

I was lying on my side, my left side. The top of my pajamas was open, perhaps he had opened them, perhaps it was just a hot September night. His thin arms were around me, I could feel his naked chest against my back. His long arms were around me, his thin beautiful hands rubbing up and down my body.

He had the family hands, his mother's hands, his sister's hands, with long, thin fingers, and delicate, thin skin, narrow and beautiful hands. He bit his nails, a habit he simply dropped

one day years later, the way people go cold turkey with smoking.
I bit my nails, too, as a child. I don't do it anymore. My father
was tickling me, running his beautiful hands over my thin ribs,
down into the waistband of my pajamas, his beautiful fingers
playing over my penis and my balls as though he were playing
arpeggios on the piano, his thin arms around me, and I woke up
giggling and squirming. Moonlight was coming through the
window, thin and pale.

His left hand began to play with my left nipple, his thin fingers thrumming across it like strumming a guitar string, his long
thumb brushing and brushing until my tiny nipple rose from my
chest. His right hand, the beautiful fingers, began to play over
my lips. I was laughing softly, twisting in his arms, my head
moving from side to side.

SOMETHING TERRIBLE WILL HAPPEN. I was told that, and I
believe it. Terrible things did happen, of course, terrible things
later, but worse things are coming.

THE SLIM FINGERS of his right hand, the flesh soft and
smooth, merely a fragrant sheath for the beautiful bones, began
to open my mouth, began to play with my tongue, one and then
two and then three in my mouth. The tips of his fingers ran over
my tongue, ran over my teeth, pulled at my lips to open them
farther.

His left hand strumming, a whispering flutter, across my left
nipple, beat, beat, beat, like a hummingbird sipping at a flower,
his right hand deeper and deeper in my mouth and then it
wasn't fun anymore, it wasn't funny.

WHAT MAKES A CHILD of four realize that something awful is going to happen? Something awful in the dark? I began to know this, began to know it in my body.

HIS RIGHT HAND WAS DEEP in my mouth, reaching the thin fingers down my throat, and I began to gag. I began to squirm, trying to get out of his grasp, trying not to throw up with his hand down my throat, the round fingers of his soft hand on my windpipe.

That room. That dark room which I had to enter a thousand times again in later years. I don't go in there anymore. That room where the worst things that have ever happened to me in my life happened.

Then there was something poking and prodding at my behind, something thin and stiff and hard. My pajama top open to his hands, my mouth open to his fist, my pajama bottoms pulled down and something poking at me and then he was inside, inside my body, moving quick as a rabbit inside me, pushing and pushing, tearing my skin, small and quick as a rabbit, and he wouldn't stop strumming my nipple and his hand moved deeper into my throat and the moonlight was shining off the white door of his closet and I could see the furniture in the room, his clothes thrown any which way over the furniture, and he moved behind me, his hands in front, and he began to moan in my ear.

Something about my father. When he was sixteen, he was sent to college, a military school still known as the West Point of the South. He was, there's no other way to say it, pretty. He was delicate and bone-thin and pretty, with soft brown hair and fine features and beautiful hands. His introduction to military

life, the hazing, was, as it was for all cadets, brutal and dehuman-
izing and strident, but he made it through.

He was an athlete. He was a flyweight boxer, and he got
beaten again and again but he kept on at it. He was a runner, and
he once had cinders scraped from his knee with a horse cur-
rycomb after a fall on the track.

His years at VMI were some of his happiest memories, before
everything, when he was still just a pretty child.

When he was in the war, he once sent a picture to my mother:
my father standing in a combat helmet standing on a beach. On
the back he wrote, in his beautiful handwriting, "I don't remember much about taking this picture; I just remember how badly
I wanted a drink."

I could smell his hot bourbon breath. I could feel the beard
on his cheek, the stubble sharp now in the night. He was whispering to me, calling me his darling maybe, whispering words I
don't remember. My legs were restless as though running and
the pain was sudden and startling and excruciating and I couldn't
get away, could not run away from the hand on my nipple or the
fingers down my throat or this strange hard thing inside me.
My father.

My father was a handsome man. As a child in the twenties, his
blond hair was cut in a kind of pageboy style, as though his
mother wished she had had a girl. In photographs, he always
looks fine. He has perfect posture. Somewhere in all of this, there
is the pleasure of being held by my handsome father, somewhere
in all of this there is the moment at which it all began, the sensuality, the desire, even the willingness to hurt myself later, years
later, because it was the only sensual experience I had at hand,

because I could not bear to imagine being touched with love or affection by another human being anymore, and cutting was a kind of affection. It all began in that dark room with the moonlight, with his hands. Somewhere in the pain there is pleasure, and that is the most awful part, perhaps.

The moonlight was coming through the window. I could see the door of his closet where he hung his smart clothes, where he hung his uniforms, the raw sweat smell of the woolen cloth, the uniforms that he wore to teach, the smell that never went away, the smell that all the men and all the cadets left behind them when they left a room.

He had shoes that had belonged to his uncle who was in the legislature, fine old brown leather shoes. He had white bucks he kept immaculate with a solution that came out of a bottle. Sometimes he let me make his bucks white again, cover the grass stains and the scuff marks so they were perfectly white and unmarred in the summer sun. There was an old gun in the closet, although he didn't hunt, changed the subject to something else when the men talked about ducks or deer. Maybe the gun didn't even work. It disappeared and we never knew.

He was inside my body and the pain was enormous and the moon was coming in the room and I was wearing striped summer pajamas and I was gagging because his long thin fingers could go so far down my throat. He held me tighter to him. I could feel the fine brown hair on his chest, his thin legs between mine, forcing them open. He pulled the bottoms of my pajamas down farther so they were around my ankles, and I couldn't speak or cry out because my mouth was full of his hand and the fun was all gone now, whatever pleasure there had been was killed, all forgotten, and I was afraid and in pain.

He was thirty-five years old. His hair turned dead white by the time he was forty, beautiful fine white hair. He was born in 1917. When he was four he looked like a girl. He was thin, not just his hands but his whole body, and there was bourbon, sick-smelling liquor on his breath and in my ear and the house was filled with people, people in every bed, people sleeping, and there was nowhere to go and my aunt was getting married the next day and so there had been a party with a lot of drinking and laughing even though my grandfather was dying upstairs and knew it and I couldn't get away. I was four. He was five-foot-eleven. I barely came as high as his thigh.

The next time you're walking down the street, look at a father walking with his tiny son. Just take a look.

I turned my head, the hot tears on my cheeks, trying to get his hands out of my throat, but my arms were pinned by his arms around me.

He told me later that he had decided as a child to be like the Spartan boy who let the fox eat out his entrails. Because his father was a drunk. Because, as a teenager, he had to drag him home from saloons, go get him when he had smashed another car. Because he had a miserable childhood, I suppose.

When I turned my head, I could see my mother, on my father's other side. She was just coming awake, murmuring in her sleep and opening her eyes, her party makeup still on, her lips black in the moonlight, her nails black, her nightdress transparent in the weak white light. I could see the curve and shape of her body, could see the curve of her breasts as she sat up and held herself up with one arm. She looked.

She screamed my father's name, and she raised her free arm straight up to the ceiling and slapped him just once, on the shoulder. She said his name once. And she slapped him once. She slapped him hard, I could hear the smack on his bare skin.

And he stopped. His fingers stopped moving on my nipple, his fingers came out of my mouth, and I felt the soft suck of him leaving me. He got up and went into the bathroom. My mother just sat there in the moonlight. She sat there staring as I pulled the bottoms of my pajamas up from around my ankles, as I lay shivering in the hot sheets. I didn't look at her. I turned away. I didn't cry, I don't think I was crying anymore. I just turned away and pretended I wasn't there.

She didn't touch me. She turned over and slept.

My father came back into the room, his boxer shorts baggy and white in the moonlight, and lay down next to me. Between my mother and me. He was asleep immediately. Sometimes, in the night, he would move closer, and his skin would touch my skin without menace, but still I would move away, move away until I couldn't feel the touch of his skin on mine. The casual, slight, unconscious touch of a man's skin on a boy's, the thin arms, the hair on his chest, the thin cotton of his boxer shorts, his waist already going soft, nobody cared in those days, his shoulders as he turned, his hands, slightly grazing my own sweet skin, which was ruined forever.

TERRIBLE THINGS WILL HAPPEN. Things you can't talk about. Things that bring death.

No angel came, like in the dream. No angel came to carry me into my own safe bed.

My father turned over. I could feel his thin, elegant back, the bones of his ribs, his spinal column, like a bird, he was so fine. He was dead to the world. He didn't know he was touching me. Somehow, the fact that he didn't know he was touching me made his touching me worse. I have never been able to bear the casual, unknowing touch of a stranger or even a friend.

Three figures in a bed. Three figures in a white, hot landscape on a night when the party had gone on one drink too long, when all the beds were full and my grandfather was dying in striped pajamas and something was done that could not, that could not, that could not ever be undone.

My father taught young men English history. He could recite all the kings and queens of England in order. He was a failure; he had never completed his thesis and so was an object of some pity, but he was a good teacher, and the kings and queens thing was a good trick, and he could tell a funny story, drink in hand. He was never the same, either, although I didn't know it for a long time.

The next morning there was blood when I went to the bathroom. The next morning there was fear when I thought of any part of my body.

The next morning there were Bloody Marys and the hearty laughter of young men and women who have had too much to drink the night before. People in those days had drinks in the morning because they thought it was sophisticated and comical to be hungover, like Mary Astor or Katharine Hepburn in the movies. The next morning, dresses and hats were laid out on beds, and Queen Anne's lace and magnolia leaves and autumn clematis were put in vases on the mantels after breakfast.

I sat on a sofa in my grandmother's dining room. It was small and upholstered in beige linen covered with large cabbage roses. Everything in the house was fresh, so fresh and clean for my aunt's wedding. People were bustling around, people I didn't know. It was different in those days in the country. You got married in a church and had a reception at the house, with Mrs. Cake Agnor, that's what she was called, making the cake, and country girls to pass the sandwiches, and black men in white coats to pour the champagne.

In those days it was simple. It was sweet, and it was a simple and sweetly happy occasion. Just cucumber sandwiches and ladies in hats and short white gloves and a bride who glowed with pride and joy.

I sat on the linen sofa while the women moved around my house, my grandmother's house, fixing sandwiches, laying out the tablecloths, and I told her what had happened. I told her everything, the night, the bloody morning, everything. She must have been so distracted. Her husband dying upstairs, her daughter being married and so much to be done, and a four-year-old boy with a distasteful story to tell.

My mother used to say that when I began to talk I talked so much she turned to me one day when I was four and said, "Do you have any idea how much you bore me?" She used to tell that story all the time.

But I told my grandmother, and she listened, and then she said, "Don't ever tell this story to anybody else. If you tell this story to anybody else, something terrible will happen. Something terrible will happen to our family." And then she had a lot to do.

MY FATHER DROVE my aunt to the church. He walked her down the aisle in a white jacket and gave her away. He gave her away because her own father was dying. My mother stood beside her sister in a rose dress and hat and looked serene.

I'm told that, on the way to the church, my father stopped the car and got out and threw up on the side of the road. My mother always said he had a hangover.

The rest is just a life, just the story of a life deformed. The rest is just a life in which nothing else, no other moment, really matters.

I don't know if it ever happened again. I think it did. I don't know if it ever happened to my brother or sister, but I don't think so.

I think it was just an accident. I think it was just bad luck. But afterward, my mother and father and my grandmother and I were locked forever in a secret, each knowing, each silent. I don't know how they felt. I don't know how something couldn't have been broken that was whole, how something that was lovely could ever have been lovely again.

It happened to me on a September night when my parents were drunk, and I never forget it. Every time I looked at my father, I could feel his hands on my nipples and his fingers down my throat.

I went on. I pretended to be a child. I knew I was pretending to be who I was; I was constructing a good-humored fiction so that I might appear to be the way other children seemed to be: polite, winsome, and funny. I didn't feel like I was any of these things. I felt I was copying the smiling face, that I was an imitation. I was a faker, and a fake.

She knew. She had seen it. He knew. He had done it. My grandmother knew. It had been a full stop in the music of a happy day. And I knew and I could talk and I could tell. And so they werc afraid of me, and took their revenge later in extraordinary scenes of hatred. I don't think they ever knew that I had told my grandmother, on the day of my aunt's wedding.

How did we go on?

I know I wanted my parents to like me. I wanted them not to be afraid of me. I know I wanted us all to be safe, and we all knew we weren't. We knew we were lying all the time.

I am told my father screamed at me in public. I am told he called me a pig. I am told he screamed that I ruined everything nice. I am told that their friends begged them to buy me a bicycle like my brother's, even offered to lend them the money. My brother had one. My sister had one. I don't remember any of these things.

I knew, I always knew, that one day I would find somebody I loved enough to tell this story to, and years later I did, one cold morning, lying in bed naked in Philadelphia while his wife was away at work, I knew I had found somebody I loved with all my heart, and I told him the story. I told every detail.

In the telling, I thought, would be the expiation; but it didn't make one bit of difference. It didn't make one goddamned bit of difference.

When I was twenty-two, when I was in love with my first

real girlfriend, I made an appointment with a doctor I'd never been to. I told him I was convinced I had a sexually transmitted disease, that I might have given it to others. He asked me what symptoms I had, and I said none. He looked at me oddly, he looked at my penis, he held it in his hand and looked at it, and I was afraid for him, touching it, I was sure he would see it, that there would be visible proof of some raging infection, but he said nothing. He gave me a blood test, a Wasserman, and called two days later to tell me that all the results were normal. I was perfectly healthy. Of course. He must have thought I was insane.

And it didn't make one bit of difference, not one goddamned bit of difference.

A drunken bed in the white-hot dark of a September night with my grandfather after whom I was called dying three doors away. My father, my mother, and me. My father fucking me in the night. My mother watching. It's a sad story for everybody.

I live alone now. I have lived alone for twenty-five years. No one touches me, there are no lips to kiss. Once a doctor asked me if I snored and I had to say I didn't know. I was at that moment humiliated by the whole history of my life.

EVERYTHING IS DARK NOW. Something terrible will happen.

My mother was beautiful, my father handsome. He had such charming hands, my father.

Such charming hands.

The End of the World as We Know It

It wasn't even what happened. That was bad enough. It was what happened after. That was worse.

My mother was sitting with her friend Sunshine, who wasn't a nurse or anything but who worked in a hospital, and I was still very young, in kindergarten probably, at my little private school run by the woman whose son was a lunatic, at least only half a day of school, and I was home and they were sitting there having coffee or maybe early drinks, while Sunshine complained about her husband the drunk, and I came into the room and said, "There's blood when I go to the bathroom."

My mother made me take down my pants and show Sunshine. My mother said, "She works in a hospital. It's probably just something you ate." With my pants down around my ankles, showing Sunshine my rear end, Sunshine pulling my cheeks apart for a closer look, my little hole, bloody. Something I ate.

I started first grade and after a few weeks my mother asked me if there were any girls I liked in my class. We were standing in the kitchen. I said sure, and named a few. Then I said there were some boys I liked, too, and I named a couple.

My mother turned on me and said vehemently, "Just make

sure you like the girls better than the boys!" What could she have meant, except that she knew, she had been there and she had seen?

I was a little whore. I was a whore and I fucked grown men, I let grown men fuck me. What else could she have meant?

She called me Robbietydabobity the big fat hen. It was her term of endearment for me. Hen. I never understood, when I thought of it later, how she had come up with that, what she meant by it.

When I was ten, I watched a friend of my brother's masturbate, sitting on the edge of one of the ancient rock pools, down where the creek runs into the river. He pulled down his bathing suit, he made his penis hard and big—it was the first time I'd ever seen a penis except my own—and then he masturbated until white come shot all over his brown stomach. He told us the word for it.

I was electrified, at the size of his penis, at the pleasure it gave him, at the expressions on the faces of the three other boys who were watching. He was not embarrassed. He was teaching us the way to a grownup pleasure, and he took pride in his ability to demonstrate. He had a lean, smooth brown body, and there was stiff brown hair on his head and under his arms and around his penis.

It was high summer, late afternoon. The heat and the light just sat on you; not a breath, as my grandmother used to say, making a particular gesture with her hand as though slowly batting away a fly, not a *breath*. The back-to-school cicadas were singing in the limp willows.

I sat and watched while the other boys practiced what they

had learned. I saw the looks on their faces. I was too little, I was ten, a child in a grownup world.

Watching my brother's friend, I wanted to know what it would be like to be so handsome, to live in such a beautiful fourteen-year-old body, pure and untouched by time, by sadness or disappointment, untouched, and to be able to give myself such an infinite pleasure.

Once, in Rome, I had my hair cut and bought a maroon knit shirt and one of those bags called *borsa* Italian men carry, thinking it would make me dark and romantic like the Italians. I thought, I'd rather be blind and a beggar than be an ugly man in Rome.

My father never talked about sex. We never saw him naked. My mother would come in and go to the bathroom while we were in the bathtub; we never watched, but we heard her, pulling down her girdle, the quick shush, the sharp smell, peeing, the straightening of the garters that were attached to the girdle to hold up her stockings, straightening her dress, checking her hair, her lipstick, casual. But not my father. He peed out the back door, in the dark, even in the winter. We knew nothing about sex, except what we learned reading the dirty parts of *Lady Chatterly's Lover* in secret.

My father had the longest testicles I've ever seen. When he came out of the bath, they hung down below his boxer shorts. We never, ever saw our parents naked. My mother used to say there was nothing disgusting about the human body, but we were never naked.

So watching the brazen, unashamed behavior of my brother's friend was magical. The next morning, lying in my summer bed, with my thumb and forefinger, I pulled on my penis for half an hour, my bare, bald, tiny child's penis, until I felt the rush of pleasure, and found my eyes squeezing shut the way my brother's friend's had.

I was tired of being a child. I was tired of pretending to be innocent, of pretending to be funny and winsome and smart and endearing.

Somebody once told me that I was the only child she had ever known who always turned the conversation away from myself, to ask how others were, what they'd been doing, complimenting them on some part of the way they looked. It was because I didn't want to talk about myself. It was because I had no self to talk about, because I didn't want to be asked any questions, out of fear that any question would lead to *the* question and the answer would be yes and everything would be ruined and something terrible would begin to happen.

I didn't want to be a child, to stand in that relation to the world in which I was continually vulnerable to attack, no matter how much I pretended to be fine. No matter how much I said it before I changed the topic. I didn't want to be winning. I didn't want to look the way I looked. The way I looked was so different from the way I felt, from what I knew to be inside me. I had the soul of Mahler and the body of Mozart. I didn't want to be me.

I wanted stiff wavy hair and stomach muscles and a long lean torso. I wanted to be a boy who was strong and untouched and able to give myself pleasure, and to dream of the day when the prize and the flowered cock would be mine, like in *Lady Chatterly*. I didn't have a good body until I was in my late thirties, after I got out of the mental hospital, and even then it seemed less beautiful, less prone to pleasure than the body of my brother's friend by the river, his hand around his dick, his eyes dark with sensation.

So I would think of my brother's friend and his pleasure, and the thought gave me pleasure, and I would masturbate in bed, terrified of being caught. I didn't know what would happen if I got caught, but I liked the secrecy of it, the fact that it had to do only with me and what gave me this thrill of pleasure, this sense, for a moment, of no longer being a child.

It was the only moment I wasn't faking. It was the only moment I didn't have to be something for somebody else. It was the moment I could have any body I imagined. I stopped thinking. It was the quiet, intense moment in which I could see, with absolute clarity, without thought, the handsome body of my brother's friend, leaning back on one muscled arm, the water spilling over his hand, the come shooting over his brown stomach, his tan line, his bathing suit floating in the water, his nipples erect and dark. I could feel the awe on the older boys' faces as they learned the mystery; they could see the mystery in the rush of blood to his cheeks, the high red pulse of his cheekbones.

Afterward, my father never touched me, unless he shook my hand. Except once, later. He never held me or kissed me or tousled my hair. He never took my hand as we walked up the steep steps to the church where he stood against a stained glass window and sang in his high sweet tenor voice the ancient hymns of the Episcopal Church, holding the hymnbook in his long hands, his summer seersucker perfectly wrinkled, his face a masterpiece of calm, no matter how hungover he was. And he must have been. He could hold his liquor, then, but there was season after season when they all drank too much. It was what they did.

One day, when I was masturbating, I noticed a small deposit of something white beneath the thin skin. For days, I hoped it would go away. I squeezed and squeezed it, trying to make it disappear. It didn't.

I knew, finally, that I was going to die, that something had happened in that bed with my father eight years before that would kill me. And I knew that I could kill others. I knew that whatever disease I had gave my touch the power to make others sicken and die. It was sex. The terror of sex. It came to me all of a sudden.

The white spot on my penis broke up into many similar, smaller ones. Sometimes I would squeeze and a tiny amount of white wax, like a worm, would come out. Sometimes I would squeeze so hard and uselessly and repeatedly that a boil would develop, a boil that eventually erupted in blood and pus. Disease made tangible, blood in my fingers. And I began to come.

I dreamed I reached into my pants and pulled out my testicles. They were white and mottled. They were pitted like a sponge.

I dreamed I took a spoon and dug long white worms out of my knees. I dreamed these things again and again. They terrified me until I felt nauseated.

And still, I would masturbate six or seven or eight times a day, in any room of the house, at any moment when I knew I would be alone. And most times, the masturbation would be followed by a sharp searing pain, a pain that made my penis feel as though it were on fire, as though a hot wire had been inserted down through the middle, a pain that was so intense it would make sweat come out all over my forehead. Sometimes, if I could make my penis hard again right away, it would pass in ten minutes. At other times, it would last half an hour or more. Sometimes I was late for dinner, lying sick with sweat and pain on the bathroom floor.

It was part of my disease; it was a symptom of the thing that was killing me, this sexual thing that had come into my body through my father's touch. It was in the pain. It was in the white spots, small hard clots that dotted my penis. It was in my mother's accusation when I was five. It was in the way I had faked a childhood.

But I couldn't, I wouldn't stop. I was both victim and victimizer. I was possessed. My greatest pleasure, my one private pleasure, was also death.

At first, I was terrified of dying. Then I found that all I wanted was death, to end it, to keep myself from spreading the infectious toxins that ran in my veins. It was a poison that would find its way through me into the body, the bloodstream of any other living person. I was thirteen years old, and all I thought about was death. I believed my touch could kill, that every touch put another person in danger.

Of course, there is a certain gladness in being young. There is an exhilaration in watching your body change, in leaving the helplessness of childhood behind. There is the pleasure of friendships that have nothing to do with your parents, the brilliance of even the earliest ideas about the world, about the mind, the art of conversation, and none of this was lost on me, even though I did not turn lean and strong, I did not turn beautiful; I was instead skinny and awkward with bad posture and a weak chin.

I once asked my mother when my face had changed, how I had come to look so sad. We were sitting in front of the liquor store, waiting for my father.

She looked at me in the rearview mirror. "You decided," she said. "You decided to be sad." I was twelve.

My hair did not bristle with stiffness, the way a man's hair should. It was a nondescript brown, not deep, not rich, not romantic. It was straight and fine, and lay against my head like a girl's. Everybody said I had a brilliant mind, and this, I suppose was to compensate me for the indelible pain and the homely face and weak body.

But it didn't. I knew what a man was; I knew I wanted to be one. And I knew I wanted to die because of the pain and the infection and because my body would never in any way resemble the body I wanted for myself. I had seen it once, down by the river. I wanted it to be mine forever. Instead, there was only an adoration of a self I was never going to be, and a loathing for the self I was.

I couldn't stand the casual touch of strangers or the affectionate touch of friends, the arm across the shoulder, the pat on the back. My father and his friends used to put their arms across each other's shoulders, when they were being photographed. It was terrible. I was afraid for them, for the strangers and the friends, and every touch was the touch of my father in the dark.

I didn't like my face. I didn't like my voice. I didn't like being the kid in gym class who couldn't climb to the top of the rope.

In swimming, when we swam naked on Saturday mornings at the Military Institute, under the instruction of cadets who lifted weights and had shoulders and stomach muscles and arms and thighs and the slim waists of boys, I was mortified. I would never be one of them, with sharply handsome cadet faces and crisp lines where the sideburns were shaved razor-sharp.

The lights from the high windows glittered on the infinite tiny waves of boys splashing, the deep turquoise aquatic dream of water, so clean and cold, the men and the boys swam without embarrassment and called, their shouts echoing in the high steel-raftered ceiling into which the platform we jumped off of rose fifteen feet, and I jumped with them, unafraid, I did these things and I was not afraid. In the showers, I turned away in shame. In the whole Athenian dream of what it was to be men together and strong and handsome, I was the one thing that did not belong. I was the one thing that would never belong anywhere.

I imagined there was a button buried in my thigh. I imagined a button I could push and cease to be, cease to be in such a way that I would never have been at all. There would be no funeral, no gravestone, no memory of me. I imagined a thousand times pushing this button and the world and its wonders and its joys and its compassion would vanish into invisibility.

I didn't want people's grief and tears. I didn't want to be missed. I wanted to have never been on the beautiful round whirling extravagantly peopled planet.

I broke my arm, falling off a horse named Thunder, going over a two-foot jump. There was a cast up to my shoulder. My father decided he was going to bathe me, and he made me undress while my brother watched and made me sit naked on the edge of the bathtub, while he rubbed soap over my body, under my arms, lifting my cast, hurting my arm, rubbing soap over my penis, while my eyes stared at the porcelain of the tub and I didn't move a muscle. Then he rinsed me off with a wet washrag, and toweled me dry. It was the last, the only other time he touched me.

A boy named Roy lived across the creek from us, with his grandparents and his aunt and uncle and his retarded other uncle. I was never sure where his parents were. He was sixteen, with jet-black hair and white skin and an open country face. My sister adored him. One of her favorite games was to get me to help her turn over her swing set, so we could stand at the edge of the creek and call for Roy until he came over and set it back up for her. He was good at it. He looked like the kind of boy who would get to be a man who would be good with tools, who would be covered with grease from fixing other people's things.

They were a kind, simple, warm family. I liked being with them. The aunt made the best biscuits in the world, dripping with country butter. They had an outhouse. They ate their big meal in the middle of the day, roasts and chickens and ham and four vegetables served at their round table next to the woodstove. I spent the night there sometimes. I would often eat with them and go home telling all about the biscuits, which drove my mother crazy, since she was famous for making great biscuits. She asked the aunt how she made them. She said she made them out of a box of Bisquick, while my mother made hers from scratch, so my mother bought some Bisquick and followed the instructions on the box. They still weren't as good. It turned out, after several trips by my mother across the creek, after she made Mary make her some to taste, it turned out it was the butter.

They were clean. The whole family was clean, although they

had no place to wash, except a big washtub on Saturday nights. Mary used to babysit for us with her husband, Andy, until my mother decided they'd stolen enough silver. Grandpaw was feeble but a hard worker, and Grandmaw was fat and smelled of asafetida, a balm she wore in a small bag around her neck. I don't know what for.

Part of the way they made their living was that the retarded uncle, Henry, would collect empty pop bottles from the side of the highway, on endless round-trips to and from town, and the family would return these for the two-cent deposit. Every Saturday morning, we would spend hours washing the bottles with a scrub brush, washing them inside and out, so that Mr. Russ at the general store wouldn't think they were dirty rednecks.

Between our houses, there was a wide field covered by dense trees and undergrowth. It was our endless private playground, so dense that in the high summer you could not see Roy's house from ours. It had a small meadow in the middle, not visible from either house. The meadow was covered with old empty cans of engine oil, and we would pour the excess from the cans and try to start small fires. There was a dark, dense place where grapevines grew into an arbor, a private arch I would crawl into, hidden from the world, and masturbate in the damp half-light.

One day my brother and I were in the field, lying in the tall grass with the rusted oil cans looking at the sky. Roy joined us.

"I've got a date tonight," he said. "She's ready. I know it. We're going to do it. Tonight."

He had our attention. Just the thought of doing it with somebody, of skin on skin in the back of a car, in the dark tall grass of a field, out by the river on a broad smooth rock.

"Just wish I had somebody to practice on. Yeah. I'd like to practice on somebody right now."

I turned over on my stomach. I undid my jeans and slid them down. "Here," I said. "Practice on me." It was the summer I turned thirteen. He came inside me.

My brother watched. We never spoke about it ever again, afterward.

Roy never said a word about what had happened. We never knew what happened on his date and, when he moved away not long after, we didn't know where he had gone and we were getting older and more sophisticated and Mary and Andy had stolen the silver butter plates and we didn't go see Grandmaw and Grandpaw so much anymore.

I don't know whether any of these people are still alive.

Every part of my being was sexual. When I turned thirteen, I was four-foot-eleven, but changes were starting in my body, and soon I could come across my naked stomach, an orgasm followed by the searing burning that the boy, my first handsome instructor by the river, would never know. He would go on to take for granted the pleasures of his body, he would have sex with women, he would have children who would be whole and healthy and happy and untouched in their beds. These things would not happen to me.

My children would be deformed monsters. They would be spongy balls of pus. I would violate their innocence in the dark. Their mother would die.

One day a friend of my sister's was out to play. She was eleven. I found her alone in the sitting room and, wordlessly, I knelt beside her where she sat on the sofa. She knew what I wanted. I wanted to touch her. I wanted to touch and kiss her and hold her and believe for one minute I was one of the cadets on Saturday mornings with hair on their chests and long thigh muscles that moved as they dived off the high board. I knelt beside her, knelt on the floor beside the sofa, and slowly slid my hand toward hers. I touched the little finger of her hand with the little finger of mine and I came in my pants and I was afraid for her and I ran from the room and I never touched her again.

For years, I waited for word, afraid for her. I was afraid to hear of her death, of the boils and running sores and searing pain inside her.

Anyone could have told me I was mistaken. Anyone could have told me it was not my fault. But I didn't tell anybody, for fear of the terrible thing that would happen. That thing will happen now.

I just wanted to touch. I just wanted to be touched.

My grandmother, my father's mother, Jinks, had a small summer cottage on the Potomac. We would stay there a lot in the summer. One year, my brother and I took along the boy who had masturbated down in the creek.

Next door lived a blond, athletic girl, a year older than I was, and she and I would ride out in the evenings, every evening after supper, across the tarmac and down the dirt roads that led through the creeks and the swamps of the big river. As we bicycled through all the dense heat, heavy with sweat, when the bees circled crazy drunk around the rotted apples lining the road, in the long summer twilights, she would sing me saccharine religious songs as we rode along. She had an amazing voice, rich and throaty.

It was a small house. I don't know where everybody slept. The grownups would stay up much later than we would, having fun, and they would always be up in the morning, so I don't know where they all slept or how many beds there were.

There was a portrait of General Nathan Bedford Forrest hanging in the living room. Every night we would eat crabmeat and tomato sandwiches. That's all we ever ate, it seems like.

The boys slept in a screened-in little guest cottage that had one room and a bathroom and a wide sleeping porch. The boys would all shower together after swimming, and one day we were horsing around and knocked the top off the toilet and I cut my foot really badly, right across the heel. I still have the scar.

We were miles from town and a doctor, so my mother bandaged it tightly and I hobbled around and stayed out of the river the next day. The next night, after supper, the athletic blond girl called me to go for our ride, and I went. I wanted to hear her sing, "He can stem the tide. . . ."

On the way back, we noticed that blood was seeping through my bandage. We stopped to rest, and we lay down in a soybean field off the road. The plants were up over our heads, when we lay back.

She kissed me, and then she kissed me more urgently, she put her tongue in my mouth and my tongue slid over her slick teeth and then she pulled down her shorts and then she pulled down mine and she stuck me inside of her. I was thirteen. She was a year older. I didn't even know what was happening.

When we were done, there was blood all over her legs. I didn't know what it was, but I knew it was something terrible, something I had caused. It was blood from my cut. She washed herself off in a creek off the river before we went home.

I told my brother and his friend what had happened, lying in the mosquitoed dark of the sleeping porch. They didn't believe me. I told them again. I described it. They said prove it.

The next day, after swimming, we took the girl next door into the boys' sleeping cottage and there she took off her bathing suit and I did too and we got shyly under white sheets and we did it again. My brother and his friend sat on the other single bed and watched us.

My brother watched me do it with the girl next door.

The next winter, my grandmother got sick and died. The cottage was let go of, and I never saw the girl again. I heard she worked in a bank when she grew up.

There's only a little bit more. There's not much more except more of the same. There's driving a beautiful girl on a dark night out to the river, a blond and lovely girl who had slept around and who had chosen me, for no reason, for some reason of her own knowing, or just simple hunger, maybe, and lying with her next to the river and not being able to touch her. Going swimming with her in my underwear in the black night, out in the black rocky water of the river, she in her bra and underpants, because I was too afraid of being naked, I was so thin, and she was embarrassed for me, too afraid of being aroused and touching her.

I have regretted that moment all my life. To think of it. The touches not touched. The kisses given in fear. The sex that did not happen, again and again and again. The sex that did happen, the sex I think about every minute of every day. The ease with which other men wear their bodies, the urgency of their honest desire. Or so I imagine. So I suppose. The whole sensual life that was all I ever cared about that passed me by. That I let go of. Let go of hoping for. The life of the flesh and its pleasures. The silence in which my life has passed.

Just a little bit more.

He was tall and lean, with a big chest and broad shoulders and coal-miner's hands. The dense, close beard on his face grew in perfect lines, so that, when he was just shaved, he looked as though some careful artist had shaded his face with a brown pencil. He was four years older than I was, he was twenty-one, and we met by accident and I fell in love with him. He fell in love with me. He kissed me once on the forehead in a dark room, the room where he lived. The room was hung with multicolored gauze curtains. It was late, very late at night and raining, and he had just told me the story of his father's death, of the cruelties of his youth. He was an artist and a romantic. We both smoked cigarettes. It was the spring of my senior year in high school.

He smoked beautifully, dragging long and deep on the Lucky Strikes we all smoked then. He was handsome, even though his ears stuck out. In fact, he was beautiful in the way that only young men of that age can be, in full obedience to his passions, in full control of his body and its gracefulness. The clarity of his desire would fade in time, probably, but it had a pinpoint accuracy then. He loved women, and he loved to possess them. In high school, he had fathered a child that had been put up for adoption; he was to father another with the girl out by the river, a baby also returned to oblivion and, perhaps, to love.

Everybody loved him for his beauty, for the deep resonance of his voice, for his soft Southern accent and his longing eyes. He was like Patroclus, adored by Achilles. And he loved me with a blinding light that didn't interfere in any way with his absolute hunger for women.

I had never been in love before. He kissed me on the forehead and told me he loved me, and I burned with both love and shame. I didn't know what he meant. I didn't know what he wanted, or why he wanted something of me.

He was the kind of man I would never be. He had the kind of body I would never have. And he loved himself in a way that I would never know, even for a minute. If I had been handsome like that for fifteen minutes in high school, my whole life would have been different. On prom night. On a fall evening when men in short jackets burned leaves in the yard. On a night by the river with a blond girl whose name alone still brings a flush of shame to my face.

We talked for hours. I don't remember what we talked about. Surely we talked about love.

We lay on his bed in the dark, his arms around me, his face close to mine. I could feel his beard against my neck, a day's growth scratching. I could smell the nicotine on his breath. He said, "I wish I was queer so I could screw you." He said he loved me. In an hour, he was in the arms of the woman he had chosen for that night. For that moment.

He was the only person I had ever allowed to touch me. I allowed him to touch me because I loved him and I wasn't afraid of him. For the first time in my life, everything was blessed by love, a love that didn't invade or burn or bleed, a love that was urgent and heated and totally imaginary.

Nothing happened.

All that spring, all that summer, nothing happened that didn't feel illuminated by love and joy. Forever, it would be what love was meant to be. It was the model for everything that happened afterward, the men secret and dark and unspoken, the women public and too candid. And part of the joy was that, in public, to my family, we were perfectly ordinary friends, close but not perversely so.

There is a delicacy and an etiquette to a secret love. There are no scenes, no fights in restaurants; there are only whispered confidences in darkened rooms, lit by candlelight, illuminated by a bridled passion.

It is unreal. It is unforgettable. His tiny waist. His immense shoulders. The length of his white torso. The sound of his voice saying my name. It is without replacement.

Still I was haunted by the fear of dying, by the fear of killing him. And still the burning pain went on and on. And yet, when he whispered in my ear that he loved me, it was a fear that calmed, a pain that was forgotten. It was wrong, he had kissed me on my forehead and that was wrong, he had said he loved me and given me an erection and that was wrong, but the fact that it was wrong made the fear more bearable. It made the fear seem justified. It made the death not just desired, but deserved.

HE LIVES NOW in the Deep South, with a young second wife, and a brand-new baby. He would be almost sixty now. He probably remembers almost none of it. If he remembers it at all, he rarely thinks about it. I think about it all the time.

Life replaces things. It replaces things once vital to you, to make room for other things in your heart. I think of him almost every day. I say his name when I pray for the people I have loved. Not for who he is now, I don't know who he is now, but for who he was then. He is untouched by time, in my prayers. In my prayers, I am untouched by time, and nothing fades.

MY FATHER'S CAR broke down. That's all it was. That's all it took. A stupid Chevy Chevette on the side of the road between Weyers Cave and Staunton, choking to half-life in the half-light of an early September evening.

The boy who loved me had asked me to drive him to the airport to pick up his roommate, who was coming back to school for the fall. The drive was less than an hour and I asked my parents and they said it was fine and we went off, the man who loved me and I, and picked up the roommate and then the car broke down.

It was fine weather. I was leaving for college in two days. Summer's back was broken, but it was still hot and the light was fading, just beginning to turn to that blue haze that makes Virginia unlike any other place, a particulate light that falls on certain summer nights, a light like a mist.

We didn't know what to do. The car wouldn't run. They tried things, of course, they tried what they had learned on old wrecks and farm trucks but they didn't know much and the car wouldn't do anything.

There was a house across a field. We walked to it and the people were at supper but they kindly let us in. People did that then. They opened their doors to strangers without hesitation. They offered them something cool to drink. They would have offered us some supper, if there had been enough. They had children, who stared at us as though we were astronauts. I called my father collect.

It was cocktail time. Their supper wouldn't be for another hour. I spoke to my father. A lot of bad unsayable things were said about what kind of a person I was, and he said he sure as hell wouldn't come get us and he didn't give a good goddamn how we got home.

We took the Greyhound bus. The man was kind enough to drive us to the station, the roommate lugging all his luggage across the field, me locking the car although I don't know who could have stolen it anyway, since it didn't work. We waited hours for the bus, and we didn't get back to town until ten o'clock.

My father picked me up at the dilapidated station. He was white, speechless with rage.

At home, my mother was in her blue bathrobe with a cocktail by her side, and they didn't offer me anything to eat, and then they started in. It went on for a long time, and I don't remember it, I don't know what was said, except that it was bad. It was all about what kind of person I was and the kind of person I was was unacceptable.

I said that the car broke down. I hadn't hit anything. Nobody had been killed. It wasn't my fault. They heard nothing. My father said he had called a tow truck, and it was leaving at seven the next morning to go get the car and I had to ride with the tow truck operator as a punishment for fucking up the car, only he didn't say that, I never heard my father say *fuck* in his life.

I was crying. I was tired and I finally couldn't stand it any-more and I was crying and I left them screaming at me and I went to bed. I don't know where my brother and sister were; they must have been there. They must have heard it. To me every-thing was silence, the kind of silence a deaf person hears, the kind of black a blind person sees.

My mother came up to bed. I heard her call my name. I asked her to please leave me alone and let me sleep, I had to get up early, but she wouldn't stop and she wanted me to come into their room. I sat at the foot of their bed and it started all over again and it went on for a long time while my father sat down-stairs pulling on a drink. She was meaner than he was. She was probably smarter, and she knew how to get to you and she got to me and I started crying again because I was tired and because I just didn't get it. I didn't get what it was all about and, as calmly as I could, I said goodnight, and then I went back to my bed.

She called my name again.

"I'm not coming in there. I'm not going to come in there again."

Pause. "Yes. Yes you are." And I knew she was right, and I got up in my underwear and went and sat on my mother's bed again. I had just started wearing boxer shorts.

She was smoking. She had one of those little tartan beanbag ashtrays by her bed, you see them in flea markets now, so every time she stubbed out a cigarette there was a small noise like a child walking on a gravel driveway, and she had a drink, too, but she put the drink down and she looked at me, pulling on her cigarette, her bathrobe off, her summer nightgown thin against her body.

"I'm going to say this once, and I want you to listen carefully. If you're sleeping with him, if you're having sex with him, I'll put you in a mental hospital and I'll put him in prison."

"What?"

"I've said it. Are you?"

I didn't say anything.

She screamed at me, "Are you?"

"No! I don't know what you're talking about!"

But I did, I did know. He had kissed me once on the forehead in the gauze-draped room and I burned with shame and fear. She knew. She knew, the way she always knew when I was going to have a migraine, she knew what was in my mind. She could see us, lying in an embrace on his bed in his candlelit room. She had seen him kiss me on the forehead, bending down and putting his hands on my shoulders and kissing me gently on the forehead. She could see that, if he had wanted to sleep with me, I would have let him. She could see that I was in love.

"Stop it. Just please stop it and let me go to bed. I'm not sleeping with anybody." And I left and she didn't call me back anymore.

It was an early September night. I was just eighteen. I wanted to love my parents. I wanted them to be proud of me and I'm told they were, although they never told me. I wanted us not to look at one another like pit vipers through a pane of glass. I wanted to have sex with a blond-haired girl out by the river. I wanted the stinging, burning pain to stop. I wanted what I felt for the boy in the candlelit room to be embraceable, not to be some ephemeral wrong that my mother could see with pinpoint clarity.

I wanted to be someone else. I didn't want to be me anymore.

I got up and drove with the tow truck to get the car. I never knew what was wrong with it. There was a going-away cocktail party for me that day, and I refused to go.

"Yes, you will," my mother said, and there was no point. No point at all. My parents had stopped speaking to me, hadn't spoken to me all day except for that.

At the party, my gentle aunt, my mother's sister, came up and put her hand on my arm. She was wearing short white cotton gloves with her sleeveless Liberty lawn.

"I know it's hard," she said. "I know it's hard." I didn't know what she meant. I didn't know what she knew.

The next day my parents drove me silently to Baltimore. They chatted, the way they always did, but it was as if I weren't there. We got to Baltimore after hours of agonizing silence where we spent the night with some friends of theirs in a great big Stanford White house in Roland Park. My parents never spoke to me, but they were charming and funny and not too drunk with our hosts. They made it appear as though we were talking just normally, and I played along.

I had said good-bye to my friend the night before. I told him nothing except that there was a big insane fight. I had impressed him with my parents' relentless cruelty. I had told him I loved him, I would always love him, so foolish, I didn't, but he had held me in his arms and kissed the top of my head and hugged me tighter and tighter until I couldn't breathe.

Afterward, he and my mother became best friends. They talked for hours. They did little art projects together. He helped her plant a new rock garden. He became one of those young men she took to herself and counseled and charmed with her wit and her grace.

But that was later. That was after. As he held me in his arms, as he kissed me on the top of my head with tears in his eyes, there was no after.

I missed him with every part of my body. It was never the same ever again, not just because of my mother but because it was all as ephemeral as gauze and things change, and eventually we fought and I haven't spoken to him for years and years and years.

The next morning, my parents kissed our hosts good-bye— they were old, good friends—and drove me to campus. They helped me get my stuff into my dorm. I silently kissed my mother good-bye. I silently shook my father's hand.

My mother said, "Do brilliantly, darling. Write soon." And without another word they left me standing there, waiting for the rest of my life to start.

A Persistence of Song

In a life, in any life, bad things happen. Many good things happen, of course, we know what they are—joy, tenderness, success, beauty—but some bad things happen as well. Sometimes, very bad things happen. Children sicken and die. People we love don't love us, can never love us. Sons die, needles in their gangrenous arms, no matter how fathers value them and try to save them from degradation and despair. We lose everything we have worked to acquire, money and houses and dreams and friends. The meat of life goes bad one day and leaves us sickened.

Still, we tend to go on. We tend to want to live, to breathe the air, to stay in hotels in London or Prague and go to the theater to see the bright, the tantalizing new thing and watch baseball on TV and fly to pleasurable places in first class on airplanes and eat dinner in restaurants and pay for everybody with our platinum cards. We generally tend to love, and to be loved. We tend to want.

We want new sports jackets in the fall and linen shirts in the spring. We want to enjoy sexual pleasure. We want flat stomachs and strong arms and whatever kind of hair we don't have. We want to live while we live, not to be inert and silent as the rocks. We want to do something with the time we have, something that will give that time a certain meaning, a certain weight.

We tend to continue. We tend to continue to gossip, to admire other men and women, to fall sumptuously, even if temporarily, in love, just for the sensation, just for the way we feel in our skin, the exhilaration, the exhaustion, the innate and delectable perfection of the first kiss, the plunge into the sublime abyss.

Even if very bad things happen.

We tend to want to love our families. We tend, in fact, to do so. We are caught in a filigree of relations, of ways of being with our families, and these ways seem both more real and more binding than other ways we are caught in the web of love. We tend to have some place we call home, and that place is defined by the place we grew up, by the way our mothers cooked dinner, by the ways we dressed as children, by the way we grew to maturity as members of a tribe that was completely and wholly unique in all the world.

Even if bad things happen.

Even if we choose to sever the ties to all we ever knew as home, to redefine the spaces we live in, the emotions that seem most natural to us, the ways we have of loving, there is a haunting feeling of loss and admiration for the people we knew first and best. Even if we never speak to them again, they are our first and purest loves. There is, for all of us, a time in which they meant the world.

Sometimes, that time lasts as long as we live. It is eternal as breath. It is changeless and deathless.

Sometimes, it ends at a very early age. Sometimes, we cannot help ourselves. Things happen.

We tend to want to hear the water from the creek flowing by as we go to sleep at night. We tend to want to hear rain on a tin roof. We tend to want to watch the sky turn into blue steel on a chilly fall evening. We will want to go on picnics, rent summer houses by the sea, to kiss, to learn French or Chinese cooking, to see the mountains across the broad brown track at Santa Anita.

We will want to be more beautiful than we are, to have better bodies, to be loved in ways the people who love us cannot imagine. In ways they can never get right, no matter how hard they try.

We will not get everything we want, but most of us will get some of it. And the things we get cannot be taken from us. They are permanent. They are on our permanent record.

I recently saw pictures of my mother as a young woman. She looked happy and beautiful, sitting down by the creek in a black skirt and a white sleeveless blouse and red flat shoes. She looked happy, and the water flowed clear by her red shoes and she had a drink by her feet. In the photograph, it is a billowing summer day. If the picture were to move for a moment, she would laugh.

She looks as though she is leading a charmed life, her hair short and dark and carefully arranged, her posture gamine, her eagerness for the charm of company clear in her face. Not just for the camera, for the world. She used to say, "A collision at sea can wreck your whole day." "It's not a tragedy, it's an irritation." That's the kind of thing the woman in the photograph used to say.

In another, she is sitting with a lovely friend, down by the creek on the same day, at peace and wrapped in the embrace of kindness and affection and the pleasure of friendship. Two pretty young women, just beginning the chore of raising children, of smocking dresses, of cooking dinners and changing sheets and of living a life in which things are taken care of, in which more is saved than is lost.

And I saw pictures of myself, holding my baby sister. I look happy. I, too, look eager for life. In the photograph I am six or seven years old. My sister is squirming out of my arms, and I am holding her, presenting her for the camera. I am a handsome child, in a striped T-shirt, my brother standing behind me, blond, buck-toothed, more serious for the camera than I am.

I look happy, even if bad things happened. In the photograph, I will look happy forever. I will never look tortured, or sad, or less than handsome. I will always wear a striped T-shirt. I will always hold my squirming sister. My brother will always have buck teeth, although they were, of course, laboriously straightened in his teens.

My mother had a necklace. It was costume jewelry, rhinestones set with fake rubies, an evening kind of thing. For dressing up. For going out. It was beautiful, in an old-fashioned kind of way, in an artificially glamorous kind of way. Like something the queen might wear, except hers would have real stones. Its intention was more endearing than its execution. It had a secret and permanent value. It was the first present my father ever gave my mother.

I still have it. We tend to go on loving the things the people who loved us loved. They are invested with soul, even if the people are long dead, even if they did not turn out to be who you thought they were. I never saw my mother wear it.

I keep it because it looks like the kind of thing the woman in the photograph would own, the woman who dressed to go out at night, the woman who sewed and kept dresses in rich shades of red and blue, who hated green, who wore dresses to show off her waist. I keep it because it looks like the kind of present a man would give to a woman he loved, a woman for whom he had higher hopes than it turned out he could deliver.

On the night my mother and father met, she walked into a party and my father turned to the man he was standing with and he said, "That's the woman I'm going to marry." He picked her out of a crowd. He knew she was the one. And he did everything he could to win her heart, that's how sure he was, then.

We tend to start out not wanting to cause damage. To ourselves or to others. We only want to give love, and be given the gift of love in return, bestowed without reason and beyond our deserving. We never know why we are loved. We tend to start out wanting to be, in fact being, happy in our beloveds, happy in ourselves.

My mother showed me great affection, most of the time. She would come in to say my prayers, and she would touch my hair with her hand and I would be completely at peace at those moments.

There is a loveliness to life that does not fade. Even in the terrors of the night, there is a tendency toward grace that does not fail us. There is a persistence of song, as one poet said.

It is the tenderness that breaks our hearts. It is the loveliness that leaves us stranded on the shore, watching the boats sail away. It is the sweetness that makes us want to reach out and touch the soft skin of another person. And it is the grace that comes to us, undeserving though we may be.

It is in the photographs of our mothers and our fathers. It is in a piece of costume jewelry, left in a drawer, in the sounds of other people making love in the next hotel room, or on the edge of a razor blade in the glowing darkness. Even in the razor in the darkness.

It is in the nostalgia for the moments we are passing through even as we pass through them, the sense of loss as each slice of time leaves us.

My father was not a monster. Even at that he was a failure. He was a man whose desires got short-circuited on a hot late drunken summer night, leaving him with . . . leaving him with I still don't know what. A sense of violence thwarted. A sense of love unanswered. A sense of shame that liquor couldn't kill. Something.

And they had born in them that night, both of them, a fear of me, of each other, of the world of illusion they had created and themselves believed in with all their hearts. It was all a terrible secret. It couldn't be helped.

It was all a cruelty suddenly and unreasonably unmasked in the dark. It was an endless and living and palpable lie, despite the seersucker jacket and the white bucks and the photographs of the happy smiling son and the cocktail parties and the going out, the always going out, to talk about books and ideas and the small-town scandals that existed then.

I believe that he did not mean to do what he did. I believe

that he did not mean to whisper in my ear. I believe, because I know, that he did not intend to drink so much. I believe that he did not mean to rob me of my childhood, of the sense of innocence and wonder that is childhood's proof, what we are left with to remember and cherish when it is gone.

I see it in the faces of young men walking home from work at night, eager for the night and its chicaneries that their bodies enter into without fear or shame. They look as though some part of their innocence, some part of that beauty, had never left them. There is a flush on their cheeks. They look as though there is someone waiting for them. They look as though it excites them, this sense of being whole that carries them through a life in which things tend to get better as they go along, except the inevitable sorrow and frustration of aging, of leaving the beautiful youth behind.

It is what sustains us through the loss and the heartache and the relentless monotony, the getting up in the morning and just getting through the day. It is what keeps hope alive in our hearts.

Losing it was everything; it was the end of something that should have gone on for a long time, and once lost it was gone forever and I was never the same. Soul murder, the psychiatrists call it, the sexual violation of children.

Unimaginably small boys. Boys whose heads do not reach to their father's waists. Girls who are no more than infants. Boys and girls whose lives are ineradicably violated. Whose trust and innocence are lost to them forever.

I do not believe he meant to change the course of that life, my life, so inexorably, to create a distorting lens through which everything that happened subsequently was viewed.

The sorrow was not in all that I became; it was in the becoming. It was not in the razor in the night; it was in the fact that my father's phantom hand stretched my skin wide while my fingers sliced into the veins. It was not in the whispered kindnesses from dark strangers, or the willingness to suffer fools gladly; it was in the wandering through the night looking for the shadowed faces, for the knife at the throat, for the ultimate assignation that would signal the end, the end of the loneliness, the end of the pretense.

If you don't receive love from the ones who are meant to love you, you will never stop looking for it, like an amputee who never stops missing his leg, like the ex-smoker who wants a cigarette after lunch fifteen years later. It sounds trite. It's true.

You will look for it in objects that you buy without want. You will look for it in faces you do not desire. You will look for it in expensive hotel rooms, in the careful attentiveness of the men and women who change the sheets every day, who bring you pots of tea and thinly sliced lemon and treat you with false deference, a false deference in which you desperately want to believe. You will look for it in shopgirls and the kind of sad and splendid men who sell you clothing. You will look for it. And you will never find it. You will not find a trace.

I bought the house in which I grew up. It is very old, and it has a name. There is the creek that still runs by it, the gardens, the lawns and the giant box bushes; there is Roy's old farmhouse through the trees, although I don't know who lives there anymore.

I will not go into the bedroom where my mother and father slept. I have taken the old bed and broken it apart nail by nail with my own hands and thrown it away. I wanted to burn it in the yard, but there would have been questions. Too many questions.

I sit and write in the room where my father wrote and paid his bills. I have spent more than half my life trying to restore that house to a splendor it never had, to make it more than it was. People seem to admire it. I think it looks like an over-dressed whore, trying too hard to please. Trying too hard to say everything is fine.

I miss the simplicity of my grandmother's white linen slip-covers, the summer slipcovers with the red piping, the simple freshness of it, like furniture on a summer porch in a country where it's always sunny. I miss my grandmother. I miss my mother, dead twenty years. I miss my father, dead fourteen, too lazy to love, too drunk to know the difference, to know what he was do-ing in the dark.

I have not told this story to the people I know and try to love. I have not told it to my family. I am afraid to tell it now.

You must wonder why I tell it at all. You must wonder at the selfishness, at the hurt inflicted, at the terrible aches revisited for no real reason.

I tell it for this reason. I tell it to you now because I'd like to think that somewhere, sometime, one thirty-five-year-old father will look at his four-year-old son and not touch him and not whisper in his ear and not put his hand down his son's throat and not invade his son's body with his own and they will both turn away and sleep in innocence.

Even one single father. One single child. That would be enough of a reason.

I tell it for the fathers. The priests. The football coaches. The Boy Scout counselors. The lonely men in secret basements. Murderers.

I tell it because that one child, that one son, will have a childhood, will grow up with hope in his heart. He will take joy in his first love, the kind of sweetness and hunger country singers like Tim McGraw sing about, in beautiful, sad voices aching with longing. Lying in the back seat of a car with rain falling on the rear window, the wipers going. The hand on skin. The taste of a tongue on a tongue. Making love wearing your watch, with the television on.

I tell it for the first time the sheets are drawn back and that boy lies down with the person he loves and he is alone with his lover and happy to be there. He will stand in the shower with his lover and every idea he ever had will vanish from his mind and every cell of his skin will thoughtlessly come into being, and never again will that skin be just the membrane that holds his body together, and those hungers will never leave him.

Because everything, every single thing is sensual, every gesture, every idea, every moment of every life. A white T-shirt. The taste of food. Holding hands. Being seen. Being famous. The young women in their summer dresses. The young men who speak longingly in low voices on their cell phones on rainy street corners late at night. The men who move through the gloomy hallways of the homosexual baths, insatiable want moving their blood through their veins, quickening their pulses. Everything that makes us desire, and makes us feel desirable. It is not a life I know, but that is how I imagine the world. Perhaps I'm wrong.

When I see, on television or in the movies, people winning

things or people kissing, I cry. My heart breaks, every time, for all that they know, for all that they will ever know and be. I cherish them for winning and kissing.

I would give anything, anything, to be the man to whom this has not happened. I cannot accommodate myself to it. In a lifetime of trying, I cannot accommodate myself to it.

AND NOW I WILL have to be that person forever.

I KNOW THAT I am not the only person who is alone in the world. I know that others sorrow in the night. That others pick up a razor and slice into their own skin, with greater or lesser success. I know that others look at their lives and see only silent failure and disconsolation, feeding the cat, checking their e-mail, doing the crossword.

I know that I am not the only person to have lived a life like mine. I am aware.

THIS IS WHAT it takes to get me through the day: 450 milligrams of Eskalith, 1,000 milligrams of Neurontin, 2 milligrams of Klonopin, 6 milligrams of Xanax, 80 milligrams of Geodon, 200 milligrams of Lamictal. They do not begin to touch the anguish and shame of being what I have been, of becoming what I have become. I take Ambien to sleep. Sometimes I take it in the afternoon, just to shut off the noise. I still sleep badly at night.

I TELL THESE STORIES because I have lied about my life to people who have been kind to me and I am tired of the lying.

I tell it because I don't want people to think that I have fucked up my life over and over and over just because I was in a bad mood.

I tell it because I have been pulling myself up by my own bootstraps since I was four years old and the effort has left me sickened and exhausted and angrier than you could imagine.

I tell it because there is an ache in my heart for the imagined beauty of a life I haven't had, from which I have been locked out, and it never goes away.

I tell it because I did wish in the graveyard, because I do wish, that everybody could be the way we were at our best: funny children, a marvelous house, the mother everybody wanted to have, the mother sitting by the creek in her red flat shoes, the adorable Dickensian father who believed in Christmas. I am not the hero of my own life, I am not Prince Hamlet nor was meant to be; I am peripheral to the whole of my family, to the whole of my small circle of friends, and I always was.

I tell it for the sorrow of lying in Frette sheets in hotel rooms in foreign countries with a razor blade on the bedside table, a talisman of my own death beside the full ashtray and the clear cold glass of water, knowing that not one other soul I love knows where I am.

And I apologize. I know that it's easier to look at death than it is to look at pain, because, while death is irrevocable, and the grief will lessen in time, pain is too often merely relentless and irreversible. A *tableau vivant* of the death inevitably to follow.

I tell it because I try to believe, because I do believe with all my heart, that there is a persistence of song.

I TELL IT for all the boys, for the life they never had.

A
Conversation
with the
Author

This has to have been a difficult story to tell. Why did you decide to write it?

That's what most people ask me. Why dredge up the past again, why redig the graves long grown over? Why go through the pain of telling this story? Why not just get over it and get on with your life?

Some asked in sorrow, some in horror, some in anger, but everybody wanted to know the same thing. Why did you write it?

Here's one reason.

I was raped as a child of four by my drunken father while my mother watched. It is the seminal moment of a damaged life and I at last had to speak out.

Here's another.

There are approximately 90,000 reported cases of child sexual abuse in this country every year. Estimates are that 80 percent of the actual cases go unreported. That means approximately 500,000 children, boys and girls, are violated every year, and nobody is doing anything about it. It is epidemic in this country, and it has got to be stopped.

There are tens of thousands of boys who have been molested by Catholic priests. They grow up, they try to live the best lives they can, but they are forever shattered.

Many grew up straight, some gay, some relatively unscathed, many damaged and drugged and alcoholic and lonely and forever broken. I wrote the book for them. For us. Every story is different, and my story is unique to me. But I wanted somehow to speak for them, for the 500,000 *every year,* for the Catholic boys whose lives and faiths were forever altered, for the little boys and the little girls, in most cases with no one to tell. No one to believe them. No parents. No friends. No police. Nobody.

The cruel silence has got to end.

Did you write this initially for yourself, or did you plan from the outset to have it published?

I wrote it for myself. I didn't think about publication. I thought about expiation.

One day, I was sitting in my psychiatrist's office, and the subject of my father's bizarre funeral came up.

It was a story I had told many, many times over the years. Always with a kind of darkly comic Southern Gothic bent, saying, don't we Southerners do peculiar things in peculiar ways. The story never failed to bring laughter to the dinner table.

Yet, here I found myself telling it again, and it didn't seem so funny anymore. It seemed horrible, lonely and tragic and the final episode in a long and hateful relationship, and I found myself bawling like a baby.

I was shocked. I went home that afternoon and started to write, to try to understand, to put finally to rest the old demons. It was like shoveling the dirt into the open grave all over again.

And behind every door there was another door, and I opened

each one, without trying, as I had always done, to pretend that everything was OK. It was, in fact, a mess, and it has been a mess from the beginning, and I knew why.

You seem to have had a very close relationship with both your parents, taking care of them until the end, yet they come under very critical scrutiny in your memoir. How did you feel about that?

I loved my mother, even as she grew more pathetic. We were affectionate and intellectually in tune. She had behaved like a monster at times, but you have to understand that, from the age of four, I had this desperate need for my parents to love and forgive me. And, of course, I had a secret and cruel bond with my father, and he was so sad after my mother died, and he grew to be such a wreck, that I felt it my duty to do what I could. I used to have this fantasy that on her deathbed my mother would have a moment of clarity and tell me it wasn't my fault. I waited for that moment for years and of course it never came. And I wanted my father as he died to ask for my forgiveness, to admit some kind of guilt. He never did.

People used to ask me after my parents died, What happened? What happened to turn such a graceful, charming, and beautiful young couple into what they became, and although I had an idea, I never said anything. But, one day, I offered to tell my uncle my version of what happened. He listened to the long story in silence, and then he said, "Well, that explains a lot." That was his only comment.

I said to my uncle on that hot August morning, "I'm telling

you this, not to cause you grief and distress, not even because you asked. I'm telling you this because, if I die tomorrow, I want you to tell people that I didn't live the way I've lived just because I was in a bad mood."

You say that you had anticipated a feeling of relief if not joy at your father's death, yet you were overcome with grief. Was this a surprise to you?

It was a shock. I had wanted some kind of resolution, and now it was never to come. I had thought I would be free of the memories, free at last to live my own life with the secrets laid to rest, but I found I was locked forever alone with them. There was to be no emancipation.

At the time I couldn't have explained it all. I was just grief-stricken, I would cry at unexpected moments, and of course I was drunk most of the time, which made it worse. I just felt so alone, as sons do when their fathers die, but in my case it was a much more complicated situation than merely putting good old Dad in the ground and realizing that you have moved to the front of the line. You aren't a son anymore.

You paint a vivid picture of the fifties and sixties social life in which heavy drinking—especially at frequent cocktail parties—was the norm. How much do you think drinking affected your parents' lives, and yours in turn?

When I was little, it all looked very glamorous to me. Everybody dressed up. Everybody laughing and telling anecdotes, especially my father, who was the anecdote king. They were grownups, and

I wanted to be one, to tell anecdotes, to stand on the back terrace drinking old-fashioneds as the sun went down.

It was a life that revolved around having fun. And, for some,
the fun turned bitter and caustic. As their youth failed, and their
inadequacies were revealed, it got out of control, and then life
was not about parties and fun, it was about alcohol. It was about
blocking out regret. Regret at careers that went nowhere, at novels that didn't get published, at lives that turned sour as sheets
that haven't been changed in too long.

My parents were desperate for me to learn to drink, but I
wouldn't do it. I would fix their drinks for them, I would sit and
watch as they continued drinking long after the guests had gone
home. They drank from five o'clock until their last nightcap,
which was usually drunk in bed, but I wouldn't drink.

But when I did start to drink, at around thirty, I was an alcoholic in two weeks. And I repeated the pattern. At first I did it
for fun, to fit in with my crowd of friends, and then I just did
it to block out everything I didn't want to think about, mainly
the pain of my childhood and the endless nowhere of my adult
life.

I drank to die.

**Very self-destructive behavior became a pattern in your life.
When did that begin, and how aware were you at the time of
the underlying causes?**

When I was about fifteen, I used to imagine that there was a
button on my thigh, a button I could push and cease to exist.
Not die, vanish as though I had never been there at all, leaving

no grief, no memory, no mess to clean up. I would simply never have been. That pattern continued throughout my adult life.

And about the same time, I developed a notion that I was toxic, that my touch alone could bring infection and death to whoever touched me, that whatever my father had injected into me was in my blood, and it could kill.

It made my first romances very difficult. I loved them, but I was scared for them at the same time. I didn't want my beloved to die, or watch me die.

These notions persist to this day. Years of psychiatry, of medication and hospitalization, the death of my parents, the fact that none of my lovers have in fact died, nothing changes this idea.

I didn't know what caused it, at first, just a deep and rabid self-loathing; I didn't connect what had happened to me as a child with what I was feeling as a young adult, although I never for one second forgot it, and, again, there was no one to tell. Because I knew every question would lead inevitably back to the original question: What *happened* to you? And that was the one question I couldn't answer, couldn't even phrase to myself.

You write about the failed relationships you had with both women and men. Was there ever a time when you thought you might be able to sustain a romantic connection with someone and make a commitment to a long-term involvement?

It was all I ever wanted, all I continue to want, the coziness and spaciousness of a love that lasts. I still love every person I ever loved, I hold them in my heart with a dearness that causes me to think of them every day. I wouldn't say my relationships were failed so much as they were flawed and doomed from the start by my own feelings of self-loathing. You can fake a lot of things in a relationship, you can fake charm and generosity and passion, but you can't fake self-esteem, and because of it, I wouldn't let them in, I wouldn't let them get close enough. And it drove them crazy.

Sex is the ever-present *bête noir* of my life. I want it, I'm obsessed with it, but I'm afraid of it, too. I'm afraid of the first touch on my skin. Of opening my shirt and exposing my chest to the eyes of another human being, as though a knife would plunge deep in my heart.

So sex and relationships for me are kind of like a death wish. I'm getting better, but it will never go away.

Here's another thing: There are certain wounds that never heal, certain hurts that never leave you alone, like a broken bone that heals wrong and always twinges when it's about to rain. As a friend of mine said recently, "We always knew there was a secret; we just didn't know what it was."

You hadn't told your family or friends about the things that you reveal in your memoir—what were their reactions?

Some supported me with tremendous love and sympathy. Some stopped talking to me. The people who knew my parents well, some of my oldest and dearest friends, generally fell into the latter category. Some said I was a liar. One said I was the product of an "overactive imagination."

I knew there would be a price to pay. My parents were loved, and rightfully so. To look behind the charm and generosity to show the cankers growing inside was to risk ostracism and rejection. I have experienced both, both from family and from friends.

To tell the truth, especially after so long, is to court disaster. Supporters feel helpless to do anything to help, they know the ruin is already long past, and detractors feel the anger of watching a certain world crumble before their eyes. Of course they don't believe it. Of course they're angry, and my heart goes out to them. But there's nothing I can do about it now.

Many readers responded sympathetically to your story, but some seemed to be angered by the very fact that you revealed some of the things you write about. Why do you think they reacted that way?

I got so many heartrending letters, from people who had been abused, from alcoholics, from people who cut their own wrists in the dark, from people whose lives were completely cracked and alien to them. And, of course, you try to answer the letters, and you get into correspondences with strangers in cyberspace and you feel somehow responsible for their pain and uniquely able to listen at least to their sad stories. They are lonely. They are drunk. Their lives are wreckage around them, and they think you know some way to help them.

And so you respond and say the inane things you can think of to say, and some you never hear from again, and some become regular correspondents, at least for a time. These correspondents made me feel it was worth it to write the book, and also made me realize that this anonymous object on the bookstore shelf, my book, actually has the power to touch and transform.

A few were angry. Their general argument was that I should just grow up and get on with it. I didn't know what to say to them. Of course they're right. I *should* grow up and get on with it. I am growing up and getting on with it. And publishing the book was a necessary part of that process.

I think that, for all of us, there is a tendency to blame the victim, to say, well, you're still alive, just quit whining and act like a man. It's not that easy.

Has telling your story been a cathartic experience?

The writing of it was not particularly cathartic. I was telling a story which was known to me, in which there were no surprises, and my effort was just to tell it as simply and plainly as possible.

Having the book out in bookstores was more cathartic. Having my story be, finally, at least partly separate from me has meant that it haunts me less. I'm not particularly proud of my life; I'm not filled with wonder and self-esteem, but at least there is this book out there, my voice, speaking to people when I'm not even around, helping some of the world's damaged ones, and I'm proud of that.

What about the house in Virginia where it all took place, the house you lived in for fifty years, and the memories associated with it?

Ironically, I sold the house the same week the book was published. I'll never see it again.